320.943
T478n

DATE DUE

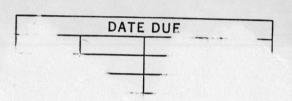

BETHANY
COLLEGE
LIBRARY

NAZISM, NEO-NAZISM, AND THE PEASANTRY

NAZISM, NEO-NAZISM, AND THE PEASANTRY

Timothy Alan Tilton

INDIANA UNIVERSITY PRESS

Bloomington & London

This volume is No. 31 in the Indiana University
Social Science Series.

Copyright © 1975 by Indiana University Press

All rights reserved

No part of this book may be reproduced or utilized
in any form or by any means, electronic or mechanical,
including photocopying and recording, or by any information storage and retrieval system, without permis-
sion in writing from the publisher. The Association of
American University Presses' Resolution on Permissions
constitutes the only exception to this prohibition.

Published in Canada by Fitzhenry & Whiteside Limited,
Don Mills, Ontario

Manufactured in the United States of America

Library of Congress Cataloging in Publication Data
Tilton, Timothy Alan.
Nazism, Neo-Nazism, and the peasantry.

(Indiana University social science series; no. 31)
Bibliography
Includes index.
1. Schleswig-Holstein--Politics and government.
2. Nationalsozialistische Deutsche Arbeiter-Partei.
3. Nationaldemokratische Partei Deutschlands (German
Federal Republic) 4. Peasantry--Schleswig-Holstein.
I. Title. II. Series: Social science series (Bloom-
ington, Indiana); no. 31.
DD491.S68T54   1975   320.9'43'51208   75-2444
ISBN 0-253-38431-1   1 2 3 4 5 79 78 77 76 75

To my family

320.943
T478n

v

Contents

Introduction   1

Chapter I.   Ecology of Political Parties in
                Schleswig-Holstein, 1919-1933   7

Chapter II.   The Social Origins of Nazism in
                Rural Schleswig-Holstein   39

Chapter III.   Changes in the Political
                Infrastructure, 1933-1970   72

Chapter IV.   The NPD in Electoral Politics   110

Chapter V.   Nazi Success and NPD Failure in
                Rural Schleswig-Holstein:
                Conclusions   134

Appendixes   145

Notes   153

Bibliography   171

Index   183

Maps and Tables

Map 1   Schleswig-Holstein   facing
                                                         page 1
Map 2   NSDAP Vote July 1932   17
Map 3   NPD Vote Bundestagswahl 1967   120

Table I-1   Percentage of Total Valid Vote
                 Obtained by Specified Parties
                 in Schleswig-Holstein 1919-
                 1933   13
Table I-2   Elections to the German
                 Reichstag in Election District
                 No. 13, Schleswig-Holstein,
                 1919 to July 1932, by Urban
                 and Rural Communities   15
Table I-3   Elections to the Reichstag in
                 Schleswig-Holstein Communities
                 with under 2,000 Population in
                 Selected Minor Civil Divisions
                 (*Kreise*), by Major Subregions,
                 1919 to 1932   18-19
Table I-4   Radicalization of "Middle
                 Class" Parties in Rural
                 Communities of Dithmarschen by
                 Subregions   23
Table I-5   Election Results in Rural
                 Communities in the Eastern
                 Hill Zone   27
Table I-6   Schleswig-Holstein:
                 Correlations between
                 Percentages of Total Valid
                 Vote Obtained in Rural
                 Communities of 18 Minor Civil
                 Divisions and Percentages of
                 All Gainfully Employed Workers
                 in Agriculture on Farms of
                 Specified Size   30
Table I-7   Schleswig-Holstein:
                 Correlations between

	Percentages of Votes Obtained by Parties in 18 Minor Civil Divisions (Cities of 10,000 or More Population Excluded) with Percentages of Population in Specified Socioeconomic Classes (*Berufszugehörige*) by Major Industrial Divisions	32
Table II-1	Forced Auctions in Schleswig-Holstein 1923-1932	42
Table II-2	Taxable Farm Income in RM per Hectare of Farmland	44
Table III-1	The Arrival of Refugees and Evacuees in Schleswig-Holstein	74
Table III-2	Unemployment in Schleswig-Holstein 1949-1952	77
Table III-3	Changes in Farm Population 1949-1965	81
Table III-4	Postwar Election Results	86-87
Table III-5	Votes According to Age and Sex	88-89
Table III-6	SPD Vote in Oldenburg 1947-1967	92
Table III-7	Persons Employed in Agriculture and Forestry in the Three Natural Regions (Communities under 2,000 Inhabitants)	103
Table IV-1	Correlations between NPD Vote and the Vote of Some Other Rightist Parties in the Postwar Period	113
Table IV-2	NPD Votes According to Sex and Age	116
Table IV-3	NPD Vote by Size of Community	117
Table IV-4	Correlations of NSDAP, NPD, and CDU Voting Patterns	118
Table IV-5	NPD Votes in Urban Working-Class Areas	119
Table IV-6	NPD Members and NPD Voting	122
Table IV-7	Profession of Head of Household and Attitude toward NPD	124
Table IV-8	Debt and Interest Loads 1968	126
Table V-1	Relations between Size of Farm and Number of Children in Schleswig-Holstein 1949	140
Appendix I	Votes According to Size of Community 1949-1972	145
Appendix II	Parties' Percentages of the Vote in Communities of under	

                    2,000 Inhabitants in the Three
                    Natural Regions 1947-1965   149
Appendix III   Economic Structure and Party
                    Vote in Major Subregions   151

Acknowledgments

For the financial assistance which made research for this essay possible I would like to express my gratitude to the National Science Foundation and the Foreign Area Fellowship Program.

For easing my introduction to research in German libraries I am indebted to the kind librarians of the Weltwirtschaftliches Institut, Landesbibliothek, and Universitätsbibliothek in Kiel, the Landesarchiv in Schleswig, and the Statistisches Landesamt in Kiel. For access to their archives and for numerous helpful suggestions the Seminar für Geschichte und Wissenschaft der Politik at Kiel, and particularly Dr. Ulrich Matthée, has my thanks. The Institut für Zeitgeschichte in Munich kindly made an important manuscript available to me. Dr. Heinz Sahner of the Institut für vergleichende Sozialforschung in Köln shared with me his detailed knowledge of voting patterns in Schleswig-Holstein. All of those whom I interviewed increased my knowledge of politics in Schleswig-Holstein, and I wish particularly to thank them for the congenial instruction they imparted to me; the cordiality of representatives of the Landwirtschaftskammer and the Bauernverband is an especially pleasant memory.

I am also grateful for permissions to reproduce material originally published in the following: Rudolf Heberle, *From Democracy to Nazism* (Baton Rouge: Louisiana State University Press, 1945, 1970); Rudolf Heberle, *Landbevölkerung und Nationalsozialismus* (Stuttgart: Deutsche Verlags-Anstalt, 1963); Rudolf Heberle, "The Ecology of Political Parties: A Study of Elections in Rural Communities in Schleswig-Holstein, 1918-1932," *American Sociological Review* XI, 1944, pp. 401-414; Heinz-Josef Varain, *Parteien und Verbände* (Köln: Westdeutscher Verlag, 1964); Heinz Sahner, *Politische Tradition, Sozialstruktur und Parteiensystem* (Meisenheim am

Glan: Verlag Anton Hain, 1972); Heinz Sahner, *Die NPD in der Landtagswahl 1967 in Schleswig-Holstein*, Diplomarbeit, Köln, 1969.

Throughout my research I have had the always stimulating and cogent advice of Dr. Barrington Moore, Jr., and the less formal but equally valuable counsel of Prof. Rudolf Heberle. I hereby absolve them of any responsibility for the shortcomings of this essay.

Vickie Robison and Dora Fortado performed minor miracles in reducing earlier drafts of this material to legible and accurate typewritten copy.

Finally, my special thanks to my favorite research assistant, my wife Mary, for her constant encouragement and help.

Abbreviations Used in this Work

Weimar parties and organizations

DDP   German Democratic Party (Deutsche Demokratische Partei)

DNVP   German National People's Party (Deutschnationale Volkspartei)

DVP   German People's Party (Deutsch Volkspartei)

KPD   Communist Party of Germany (Kommunistische Partei Deutschlands)

NSDAP National Socialist German Labor Party (Nationalsozialistische Deutsche Arbeiterpartei)

SHBLD Schleswig-Holstein Farmer and Farmworkers' Democracy (Schleswig-Holsteinische Bauern- und Landarbeiter-demokratie, or Landespartei)

SPD   Social Democratic Party of Germany (Sozialdemokratische Partei Deutschlands)

USPD   Independent Social Democratic Party of Germany (Unabhängige Sozialdemokratische Partei Deutschlands)

Postwar parties and organizations

BHE   League of the Homeless and Disinherited (Bund der Heimatvertriebenen und Entrechteten)

CDU   Christian Democratic Union (Christlich Demokratische Union)

DKP   German Conservative Party (Deutsche Konservative Partei)

DP   German Party (Deutsche Partei)

DRP   German Reich Party (Deutsche Reichspartei)

FDP   Free Democratic Party (Freie Demokratische Partei)

KPD   Communist Party of Germany (Kommunistische Partei Deutschlands)

NPD   National Democratic Party of Germany (Nationaldemokratische Partei Deutschlands)

SPD   Social Democratic Party of Germany (Sozial-
        demokratische Partei Deutschlands)
SRP   Socialist Reich Party (Sozialistische Reichs-
        partei)
SSW   South Schleswig Voters' Union (Südschles-
        wigscher Wählerverband)

NAZISM, NEO-NAZISM, AND THE PEASANTRY

Map 1

Schleswig-Holstein

DENMARK

BALTIC
SEA

Südtondern

Flensburg
Flensburgland

Husum

Husum

Schleswig

Schleswig

Eckernförde

Eiderstedt

Kiel

NORTH

Rendsburg

Rendsburg

Plön

Oldenburg

Norderdithmarschen

SEA

Meldorf

Süder-
dithmarschen

Neumünster

Eutin

Steinburg

Segeberg

Lübeck

Elbe

Itzehoe

Pinneberg

Stormarn

Herzogtum

0   50 Km
0   30 Mi

HAMBURG

Lauenburg

+–+–+ Marsh-Geest

•–•–• Geest-Hills

jmh

Introduction

This study is both an investigation into the social origins of right-wing extremism and a study of modernization. As a study of extremism it seeks to provide a careful analysis of the social basis of Nazi and NPD support in rural areas and of the effects of structural crises in agriculture in generating this support; as a study of modernization it seeks to show how structural changes in rural society have diminished, if not eliminated, the possibilities for a rural-based Fascist movement in Schleswig-Holstein. The basic argument of the study is that the material substructure of politics in rural Schleswig-Holstein (and by implication, in West Germany) has undergone a fundamental alteration that has changed the social composition of rightist extremism and minimized its prospects.

The Nazis attracted their strongest support among marginal small farmers. Now, however, the decline in the agricultural population, the increased efficiency of the farms that remain, and the possibility of subsidized emigration from the countryside have greatly reduced the numbers of marginal small farmers and eased their plight, leaving embittered large farmers, former gentleman-farmers now compelled to struggle to maintain their standards of living, as the decisive figures in the NPD's rural support. The paucity of such figures, relative to the urban population, and the greatly increased means of maintaining rural prosperity condemn contemporary rural-based Fascist movements to failure.

If this argument is correct, the social consequences are enormous. Every society that adopts economic expansion as an objective of public policy has to cope not only with the difficulties of sustaining growth, but also with the economic and political consequences of declining industries; the

contraction of the agricultural sector is only the
most obvious instance of this recurring problem.
The human misery that ordinarily accompanies the
structural crises of marginal industries can be
fraught with political implications; the petty bourgeois reaction to the economic crises of the late
Weimar Republic offers the most vivid and horrifying
example. If modern governments can reduce this
misery by recognizing incipient structural changes
in the economy, by creating new employment possibilities, and by providing incentives to accept these
new occupational opportunities, they can organize
the decline as well as the growth of industries and
can avoid dangerous political consequences in the
process.

     The theoretical inspiration behind this inves-
tigation came primarily from two sources, Barrington
Moore's *Social Origins of Dictatorship and Democracy*
and Rudolf Heberle's *From Democracy to Nazism*.[1]
Moore's work treats the growth of Fascism within the
larger context of political modernization and development. Moore argues that retarded modernization of
the agricultural sector—the failure to transform
the peasantry into some other kind of social formation—bodes ill for liberal democracy. Societies
that fail to effect a modernization of their agriculture which substantially reduces the peasant
population run the danger that the countryside may
become a "seedbed of reactionary anticapitalist
sentiment" and a potential recruiting ground for
Fascist movements.[2] Conversely, societies that do
succeed in making a successful transition to a more
commercially oriented and less labor intensive agriculture enhance their prospects for developing
stable liberal and democratic institutions. If
Moore's assessment of the social origins of Fascism
is accurate, a comparative study of the same rural
society in successive historical periods ought to
show that the threat of Fascism diminishes as agriculture loses its dominant position in the society's
economy and as the peasants make a successful accommodation to the restructuring of their industry,
either by upgrading their own enterprises or by emi-
grating to urban occupations.

     While Moore treats the sweeping historical
forces behind the peasants' adherence to Nazism,
Heberle concentrates on the particular features of
the rural milieu that explain the rise of Nazism in
Schleswig-Holstein. Heberle's work provides a

regional case study of the social elements that supported the Nazi movement. His study is more than a
careful ecological analysis of electoral statistics
that uncovers the voters and social forces that were
the bearers of Nazism; it employs interviews among
the rural population, analysis of economic conditions, and historical perspective to trace the origin
and development of the Nazi movement.

Together Moore's and Heberle's analyses allow
one to understand both the secular long-term forces
contributing to the rise of Nazism and the specific
dynamics of its growth in a particular environment.
They also invite further investigation of the fate
of radical rightist movements under different historical circumstances. In the foreword to *Landbevölkerung und Nationalsozialismus*, the expanded
German edition of *From Democracy to Nazism*, Heberle
himself suggests that

> As far as the subject of this work, the rural
> population of Schleswig-Holstein, is concerned,
> the Second World War and its consequences have
> caused decisive changes in the structure of the
> population, and thereby changes in the social
> conditions of political behavior. It would be
> exciting to build on the results of my earlier
> work and to trace the line of development to
> the present day.[3]*

The rise to prominence of a new political party
widely regarded as neo-Nazistic and as an heir to
the NSDAP—the NPD—made this replicative enterprise
even more enticing, for it offered an opportunity to
compare the development of right-wing radicalism in
successive historical periods. Not only could the
social composition of these movements be compared,
but their relative success would shed light on
Moore's theses regarding the effects of agricultural
modernization.

It was, in fact, the growth of the NPD that
provided the immediate political stimulus to this
research. During the late 1960s and the early 1970s
Fascist or quasi-Fascist movements expanded rapidly
within several of the Western liberal democracies.
In the United States the rumblings of the Wallace

---

*The author bears responsibility for all transla-
tions from the original German or French.

movement, the prospects of a disenchanted military,
and the machinations of the Nixon White House trou-
bled the political scene. In Italy Giorgio
Almirante's *Movimiento Sociale Italiano*, a party
which stressed its indebtedness to Mussolini and the
Fascist party, more than doubled its vote in the
June 1971 provincial elections, increasing its share
of the vote from 5.2 percent to 13.9 percent. But
nowhere was the possibility of a revival of Fascism
more disturbing than in the Federal Republic of
Germany, successor-state to the most vicious of the
Fascist regimes.

There, after 1965, the growth of the *Nationaldemokratische Partei Deutschlands* (NPD), ostensibly
a neo-Nazi party, stimulated fears that new political sources of human suffering would prevail on
German soil. Inside and outside the Bonn Republic,
democrats expressed their dismay at the alarming
electoral successes of the NPD. Now democratic
forces appear to have subdued the NPD; the party
seems to have exhausted its appeal and to be on the
verge of disappearing as a political force. This
rare political success story provides a further
enticement to political inquiry, for knowledge about
the causes of the NPD's demise may offer information
about the potential for Fascist movements elsewhere
and counsel about the means of vanquishing them.

The early studies of the NPD had naturally concentrated on the national party, its genesis, structure, propaganda, and prospects. Even where closer
attention was devoted to regional phenomena, the
tendency to concentrate exclusively upon electoral
and survey data prohibited a careful analysis of the
differential impact of local society upon party
recruitment. The use of this electoral and survey
data to the exclusion of other sources prevented any
analysis of the social dynamics behind the generation of the NPD vote. The social linkages, the historical traditions, and the immediate personal
concerns that drew people to the NPD did not appear
in these data; the importance of organization and
personal influence was tacitly excluded from the
list of critical factors behind NPD voting. A study
of the dynamics of NPD support that would attempt to
provide the same discriminating analysis of local
variations that Heberle provided for the NSDAP
seemed eminently warranted.

For a number of reasons Schleswig-Holstein
offered the ideal setting for a comparative study of

Nazi and NPD support. First, Schleswig-Holstein
provided an extreme case of Nazi success. In 1930
the Nazi party received 27 percent of the vote in
Schleswig-Holstein, the party's highest percentage
in any German electoral district. In July 1932,
Schleswig-Holstein gave the Hitler movement 51 percent of the total vote, thereby distinguishing
itself as the only electoral district in all of
Germany to give the NSDAP an absolute majority
before the Nazis came to power. The provincial
party achieved its greatest successes in rural districts: in 1930, 35.1 percent of rural voters chose
the NSDAP; in 1932, an astonishing 63.8 percent.

Second, knowledge about the rural social basis
of Nazism could be more complete and accurate for
Schleswig-Holstein than for any other area of rural
Germany. The researches of Heberle and his succes-
sors have provided a superbly detailed and finely
discriminating analysis of the rise of Nazism.
Heberle's efforts have resulted in the most detailed
and skillfully analyzed rural electoral data available. Subsequent studies have refined still further
his social history and economic analysis. The
archives in Schleswig contain an abundant stock of
police reports and official documents against which
the conclusions of these scholarly investigations
can be tested. (These materials on rural Nazism
provide the basis for chapters one and two of this
study.)

Third, a promising start had already been made
in gathering information on the social basis of NPD
support in Schleswig-Holstein. Heinz Sahner, following in Heberle's footsteps, had used data from
postwar elections, and particularly from the Landtag
election of 1967, as the basis for a careful ecological analysis of political parties.[4] Sahner did not
engage in the same thorough field research and historical analysis that Heberle employed, however, and
it was necessary to conduct extensive interviewing
and historical inquiry to supplement and confirm his
analysis. (These materials on rural "neo-Nazism"
constitute the basis of chapter four.)

Fourth, rural Schleswig-Holstein bears sufficient similarities to such other Nazi and NPD
strongholds as Central Franconia and Lower Saxony
that findings for Schleswig-Holstein should apply to
other regions as well. Even if these results had no
wider relevance, they would be of interest as a
bizarre and fascinating case study in extremist pol-

itics; but in all probability, developments in
Schleswig-Holstein reflect the experience of the
other Protestant farming areas of West Germany.
Heberle himself argued that Schleswig-Holstein provided a model in miniature of all North German agriculture; today Ulrike Albrecht-Waller and John Nagle
describe the dynamics of NPD recruitment in other
German villages as being remarkably similar to those
that this investigation found in Schleswig-Holstein.[5]
It is true that the Catholic peasants of Bavaria
have proved considerably more resistant to Nazi and
NPD appeals than have their Protestant counterparts,
and thus the experience of the Schleswig-Holstein
farmers may not be applicable to Bavarian conditions, but elsewhere the conclusions drawn from this
analysis should pertain.

In general, then, this study examines two
attempts to cope with structural economic crises in
German agriculture and with the political repercus-
sions of these crises. The failure of the first
attempt contributed enormously to the Nazis'
triumph; the second conscious and largely successful effort has helped restrict NPD incursions in
rural areas. More specifically, this analysis of
the NSDAP's success and the NPD's failure in rural
Schleswig-Holstein proceeds as follows: In chapters one and two I probe the social origins of
Nazism in Schleswig-Holstein. In the first chapter I review the literature of electoral studies
and argue that these studies strongly suggest *who*
voted for the NSDAP, but not *why* they did so. In
the second chapter I marshal the available evidence
to try to elucidate the motives and attitudes
behind Nazi voting. Chapter three lays out the
major demographic, economic, social, and political
changes in Schleswig-Holstein from the Weimar
period to the postwar period. In chapter four I
analyze how the NPD has fared in this changed
political context, exploring the electoral support
of the NPD and its social origins. Finally I
compare the conditions for Nazi success with the
present political environment and contend that a
strong Fascist revival is exceedingly improbable.

1: Ecology of Political Parties in Schleswig-Holstein, 1919-1933

The student of the politics of rural Schleswig-Holstein can exploit a number of intelligent studies of the region's recent political history. Of these works the first and the best are the various works of Rudolf Heberle.[1] In addition there are competent studies by Gerhard Stoltenberg (a prominent CDU politician in Schleswig-Holstein), by Peter Wulf, and by Heinz-Josef Varain, and some interesting articles from an old *völkisch* rightist, Hans Beyer. Professor Heberle set himself the task of explaining that remarkable change in the "political atmosphere" of rural Schleswig-Holstein which culminated in the National Socialist electoral victories. In his analysis of the changing relations between the political parties and the social classes of rural society, Heberle relied largely upon ecological analysis of electoral results in various subregions and in various types of rural communities. Indeed he argued that because rural people themselves write so little about their political views, the electoral record of their opinions is the best and virtually the only reliable source of information about their attitudes:

> ...All of the printed sources that we possess pertaining to the knowledge of political inclinations, and especially to those of the peasantry, must be used with certain reservations. Only in voting does the mood of the countryside receive direct and, to some extent, genuine expression; the results of elections held in

7

accordance with a secret, equal, and universal
franchise are the most exact and in any case
the only quantitative expression of political
opinion. Therefore we shall rest our case
primarily upon the analysis of electoral
results.[2]

In practice Heberle conceded the limitations of
the use of electoral statistics as a barometer of
public opinion. First, a purely statistical analysis may overstate the political conversion of individuals and ignore the impact of terror on voting
results. Heberle recognized that in small rural
communities the opportunities for intimidation and
coercion were legion, although he did not stress
sufficiently the NSDAP's employment of such tactics.
Here one recalls the observations of André Siegfried,
the founder of electoral geography. Siegfried
pointed out that even if the vote is not a perfectly
free expression of opinion, this phenomenon is
itself an interesting fact. If pressure can be successfully exerted upon a voter, a social structure
must be present which permits this effective coercion. Siegfried continued,

> That view which conceives of public opinion as
> the sum of separate individual opinions is
> totally false. In fact only those opinions
> count which are sufficiently free and energetic
> to dare to express themselves.[3]

In the closing years of the Weimar Republic democratic voters in small remote villages in Schleswig-
Holstein learned the practical truth of this maxim:
they were the group most exposed to intimidation.
The inhabitants of the cities, while by no means
free from the threat of terror, could still vote
anonymously and therefore freely.
A study confined to electoral results could
mislead in a second way, by suggesting that the
"political atmosphere" is created merely by propaganda and by the formation of individual opinion,
rather than being molded by political groups and
movements. In the Weimar Republic and in rural
Schleswig-Holstein today the close connections
between organized interest groups and political
parties constitute one of the outstanding features
of the political landscape. Therefore Heberle did
not confine himself to electoral analyses, but also

investigated the content of ideologies, the nature
of party organization, and the evolution of farm
interest organizations. I shall consider these
factors below, but here I want to summarize Heberle's
electoral analysis and then show both the advantages
and the limitations of such analysis.

Heberle begins his inquiry with the period from
1871 to 1914.[4] The thrust of his presentation is
that in the years before the First World War
Schleswig-Holstein was "a stronghold of the Liberal
and Democratic parties."[5] In 1912 the Progressives
and the Social Democrats won nine of the ten
Reichstag seats from Schleswig-Holstein, the
remaining one going to a Danish candidate from the
border area. This division of seats gives a distorted picture of public opinion, however, because
in this period the winning candidate needed an absolute majority and (as in the present French electoral system) competing parties formed alliances for
the run-off elections to promote the stronger candidate. In 1912 the Progressives' shrewd maneuvering
won them 70 percent of the seats with only 29.2
percent of the vote in the first round of elections.
In the same year the Social Democrats obtained 40.4
percent of the first ballot; in rural areas the SPD
won not quite a quarter of the votes cast. The conservative parties (*Konservative*, *Freikonservative*,
Nationalliberale) could garner only 22.4 percent
overall, a significant decline from the 41.4 percent
they had achieved in 1887. The general picture is
one of a solid liberalism, a vigorous and advancing
Social Democracy, and a weak and fading Conservatism—in short, a "rising movement for democracy."[6]

Were the rural people of prewar Schleswig-
Holstein then strongly Liberal and Social Democratic?
Heberle argues this case forcefully and contends
that "even the Conservatives were of a rather liberal denomination,"[7] but one must consider his
evidence with caution. First there is the question
of the meaning and intention behind the voting pattern, a question Heberle himself raises (and thus
moves from his original position that votes constitute a direct and immediate expression of opinion).
What interests led the rural middle classes to the
Progressives? Heberle answers the question as
follows:

There was a basic attitude of liberalism to
begin with; furthermore, certain concrete

> issues led to a clarification of political
> inclinations within the middle classes: they
> were opposed to protective tariffs on grain
> and feedstuffs...they were opposed to indus-
> trial protective tariffs....The educated or
> intellectual groups were more inclined to think
> in terms of political principles; they had been
> repelled by Bismarck's handling of the Kultur-
> kampf....They demanded an expansion of the
> rights of the Reichstag and of the Prussian
> Landtag; they were opposed to anti-Semitism;
> they also objected to the armament policy,
> partly for financial and partly for ethical
> reasons.[8]

At the same time, Heberle discerns in the Progressive ideology certain attitudes and sentiments which
later facilitated the conversion to National Socialism: anticapitalistic and antiplutocratic impulses
accompanied the anti-imperialist propaganda, and the
party emphatically rejected proletarian socialism.
Progressive party politics in prewar Schleswig-
Holstein, then, relied on a strong element of economic interest and the expression of middle-class
resentment as well as more conscientious adherence
to the liberal and democratic creed.[9] Furthermore,
these liberal and democratic tendencies derived
strong support from an opposition to Prussian cen-
tralization, an attitude that (in some areas) was
fostered by vigorous traditions of local self-
government.

In addition to the difficulties about the moti-
vation behind ostensibly democratic voting, the
electoral statistics presented by Heberle do not
seem adequate to support his conclusions. First,
Heberle's analysis of the *rural* vote is negligible.
From his data it is perhaps legitimate to conclude
that Schleswig-Holstein as a whole oriented itself
to the "Left" nationally, but one cannot conclude on
the basis of the evidence presented that the *rural*
population sided predominantly with the liberal and
socialist forces. Second, Heberle presents no
figures on electoral participation in this period.
In the 1907 and 1912 elections, just over 85 percent
of all eligible voters participated in selecting
Reichstag deputies, but this figure is misleading,
since the reservoir of eligible voters was far
smaller than it was under the Republic. Neither
women nor persons from twenty to twenty-five years
of age possessed the right to vote before 1918. In

1912, 22.5 percent of the population was entitled
to vote; in 1921, 60.6 percent.[10]
     Given the substantially smaller voting segment
of the rural population in the period before 1918,
electoral statistics may well underrepresent the
strength of conservatism in the countryside. On the
basis of the evidence the opposite conjecture (that
the statistics underrepresent the force of liberalism) is equally plausible, and the safest course
lies in arguing that the statistics for Empire and
Republic are just not comparable. When one notes,
however, that only the Social Democrats organized
carefully and propagandized steadily in rural areas
(the other parties remaining *Honoratiorenparteien*),
and when one observes that the rural population
pursued its interests—when it pursued them at all
collectively—largely in "nonpolitical" organizations like the Chamber of Agriculture (*Landwirtschaftskammer*), the cooperatives, and the local
producers' organizations,[11] then one has to conclude
that Heberle overstates the "progressive" character
of the countryside.
     The current argument does not require an inten-
sive investigation of conditions before 1918; the
point here is to retouch the picture presented by
Heberle (and by Stoltenberg) and to show that the
transition from liberalism to Nazism was not such a
startling reversal of political opinion as they have
maintained. The strength of rural liberalism has
been exaggerated and the affinity of this liberalism
to National Socialism understated. The contention
here is not that there were no honest, democratic,
well-intentioned Liberals in the Schleswig-Holstein
countryside—it is that there is insufficient
evidence that they predominated there. In this
respect the testimony of Hermann Clausen, a former
SPD leader in Schleswig who after 1945 played an
important role in the Danish party, is pertinent.
In his memoirs Clausen describes growing up in rural
Schleswig during the Wilhelmine era. In these
remote villages children learned not the values of
liberal democracy, but those of nationalism and
obedience. Clausen notes the absence of democratic
organizations, but recalls that there flourished "a
superfluity of patriotic associations that required
and cultivated submissive loyalty (*Untertanen-
treue*)."[12]
     With some reservations then about the presumed
strength of the liberal tradition in Schleswig-
Holstein, one may return to the more important part

of Heberle's analysis, the electoral evolution of
the region during the Weimar Republic. The province
lent itself almost ideally to an ecological analysis. The multiple-party system with large electoral districts and proportional representation de-
emphasized the role of personalities and electoral
alliances; instead it favored the organization of
political parties around distinct social interest
groups and thus accentuated the correspondence
between social classes and political parties. "Consequently the party constellation in any area came
very close to an expression of the class structure
of the area."[13]

Furthermore, within the province of Schleswig-
Holstein one finds a considerable variety of geographical and social structures. From north to
south through the eastern part of the province runs
the line of demarcation between the old Germanic and
the previously Slavic regions "colonized" by German
settlers. More distinctive are the three geographical regions which traverse the peninsula from north
to south—the flat fertile coastal marshes in the
west, the rolling sandy Geest in the middle, and the
Baltic hill region in the east (see Map 1). The
distinctive social structures of these three regions
facilitate a comparative analysis of the factors
which contributed to the changes in party adherence
among the rural population.[14]

In general, electoral developments in Schleswig-
Holstein paralleled those in the Reich at large.
Heberle observes three phases: the period of
Liberal and Socialist predominance (the 1919 and
1921 elections), the period of Conservative strength
(the two 1924 elections and the 1928 election), and
the period of Nazi ascendance (1930 and after) (see
Table I-1). Over the entire period one finds the
same constancy of the labor vote (KPD and SPD)—
after a notable decline in the first 1924 election—
and the same rise and fall of the conservative vote
as in Germany as a whole. There were, however,
factors peculiar to Schleswig-Holstein. First, the
Nazi upswing began somewhat earlier in Schleswig-
Holstein and was sharper than elsewhere. Second,
the Center party never had a significant following
in Protestant Schleswig-Holstein; this fact allows
one to observe even more clearly the collapse of the
middle-class parties. Third, the Communist party
had fewer adherents in this largely agricultural
province than it did in more industrialized areas;

Table I-1

Percentages of Total Valid Vote
Obtained by Specified Parties in Schleswig-Holstein 1919-1933

	1919	1921	1924 I	1924 II	1928	1930	1932 I	1932 II	March 1933
NSDAP	--	--	7.4*	2.7**	4.0	27.0	51.0	45.7	53.2
Landvolk	--	--	--	--	0.3	3.8	0.0	--	--
DNVP	7.7	20.5	31.0	33.0	23.0	6.1	6.5	10.3	10.1
DVP	7.8	18.4	12.1	14.6	13.7	7.3	1.4	--	--
Zentrum	1.0	0.8	1.0	1.1	1.1	1.0	1.2	3.5	3.1
Landespartei	7.2	3.8	0.7	--	--	--	--	--	--
DDP	27.2	9.4	8.1	8.7	5.7	4.7	1.4	--	--
Other Parties	0.0	0.7	4.6	2.9	9.0	9.7	1.6	--	--
Socialists									
SPD	45.7	37.3	24.9	30.3	35.3	29.8	26.2	24.7	22.2
USPD	3.4	3.0	--	--	--	--	--	--	--
KPD	--	6.1	10.2	6.7	7.9	10.6	10.7	13.3	10.1

* Deutsch-Völkische Freiheitspartei
** National-Sozialistische Freiheitspartei

Source: This table is based largely upon Heberle, From Democracy to Nazism, p. 94. The supplementary data for November 1932 (II) and March 1933 are taken from Statistik des deutschen Reiches.

the SPD, however, had somewhat larger than average
support, particularly in 1919 when it could capi-
talize on the pervasive disenchantment with the
regime that lost the war.

Heberle argues that the turn from the Republic
was more pronounced in rural than in urban areas:

> A comparison of the election results by rural
> and urban areas for the entire period shows
> clearly that the decline of loyalty to the
> Democratic regime was much more pronounced in
> the rural areas than in the urban communities.[15]

The figures (see Table I-2) do show that the Nazis'
eventual success was definitely higher in rural
areas, but they do not necessarily show a "decline
of loyalty." Heberle's argument is that the percentage of support for the democratic regime in 1919
was roughly similar in urban and rural areas; the
vote for the DVP, *Landespartei*, DDP, and SPD
amounted to 88 percent in the cities and 86 percent
in the countryside. The crucial interpretative
assumption is that votes for the *Landespartei* represented support for the Weimar regime. Given the
character of the *Landespartei* as portrayed by
Heberle himself, this assumption appears questionable.

The *Schleswig-Holsteinische Landespartei*, at
first known as the *Schleswig-Holsteinische Bauern-
und Landarbeiterdemokratie*, was founded in large
measure by rural people who suspected that the predominantly urban DDP would not properly represent
their interests. The party raised a number of traditional liberal demands (particularly those demands
of *economic* liberalism which served their interests;
for example, the introduction of free trade and an
end to wartime government controls on farmers). It
ostensibly supported the revolution and the Republic.
A chief spokesman and a cofounder of the party,
Willi Iversen of Munkbrarup, pointed out, however,
that

> Democracy as conceived in Schleswig-Holstein is
> something entirely different from democracy as
> represented for instance by the *Berliner Tage-
> blatt* or the *Frankfurterzeitung*. The Schles-
> wig-Holstein democracy...is a green democracy
> in contrast to the golden democracy.[16]

The party's propaganda supported a reactionary

Table I-2

Elections to the German Reichstag in Election District No. 13,
Schleswig-Holstein, 1919 to July 1932, by Urban and Rural Communities

Percentages of Total Valid Vote

	NSDAP	Land-volk	DNVP	DVP	Landes-partei	DDP	Center and Minor Parties	SPD	USPD	KPD
Urban										
1919	--	--	5.4	8.6	0.4	28.3	1.4	50.9	5.0	--
1920/21	--	--	16.2	19.6	1.2	10.5	1.9	39.8	3.2	7.6
1924 I	7.8	--	25.6	12.0	--	8.6	6.2	26.9	0.9	12.0
1924 II	2.9	--	27.8	14.5	--	9.2	3.9	32.8	0.4	8.5
1928	3.5	0.0	19.1	13.6	--	6.2	9.3	38.5	--	9.8
1930	23.2	0.6	5.3	8.4	--	5.7	8.7	33.1	--	13.1
1932	44.8	--	5.2	--	--	--	7.0	29.9	--	13.1
Rural										
1919	--	--	10.7	6.7	16.4	25.8	0.3	39.0	1.1	--
1920/21	--	--	28.6	16.1	8.6	7.3	0.6	33.0	2.6	3.2
1924 I	6.4	--	42.1	12.2	--	7.1	3.1	21.1	1.3	6.7
1924 II	2.3	--	43.4	14.9	--	7.8	2.4	25.4	0.5	3.3
1928	5.4	1.0	32.3	13.9	--	4.4	11.6	27.6	--	3.8
1930	35.1	10.7	7.9	4.8	--	2.5	11.1	22.8	--	5.1
1932	63.8	--	9.2	--	--	--	2.6	18.6	--	5.8

Source: Heberle, From Democracy to Nazism, p. 95.

Mittelstandspolitik (protection of the craftsman and
the merchant against both big business and socialism) and often conjured up the image of a romantic,
harmonious, agrarian ("green") society under a
strong leader. It called for an anti-Prussian fed-
eralism that rejected the centralized, bureau-
cratized state and celebrated instead the folk
community.[17] Stoltenberg excerpts the following
sentence from SHBLD propaganda for the 1919 elections, "Don't vote for urban party hacks and Jews
who take no interest in our little homeland, but
would abandon it to our internal and foreign enemies,"[18] and contends that previous anti-Semitic
propaganda aided the SHBLD in attracting voters.
Heberle himself considers the *Landespartei* one of a
number of organizations which prepared the way for
Nazism and he notes that the ideology of this party
"by no means represents a purely liberal but rather
a partly conservative, partly romantic conception of
state and society."[19]

The party's personnel as well as its program
render its liberalism suspect; among the notable
figures in the party was the later Nazi *Gauleiter*
and *Oberpräsident*, Hinrich Lohse. The *Landespartei*
was not a Fascist party, but it was a rural party
with an anachronistic program unsuited to an industrial era. To list its supporters among loyalists
to the democratic regime is to attribute to them a
dedication which by no means all of them possessed.
In short, not only did the rural population reject
the Republic more decisively in the end, there is
no solid evidence that they supported it firmly at
the beginning.

The Nazis' highest percentages of electoral
returns came in Geest areas. In the Schleswig Geest
the Nazis captured over 75 percent of the vote;
farther south they did nearly as well (see Map 2).
In the marshes and in the hill region their percentages declined; here the SPD and KPD had signif-
icantly stronger backing than on the Geest (see
Table I-3). The conservative DNVP had its solidest
strength among the estate owners of the eastern hill
district, but in the middle twenties they obtained
even greater percentages in the marsh and on the
Geest, a symptom of these regions' growing disenchantment with the democratic regime.[20]

Having sketched the general patterns of political evolution, Heberle turns to an analysis of
developments within each of the three major geo-

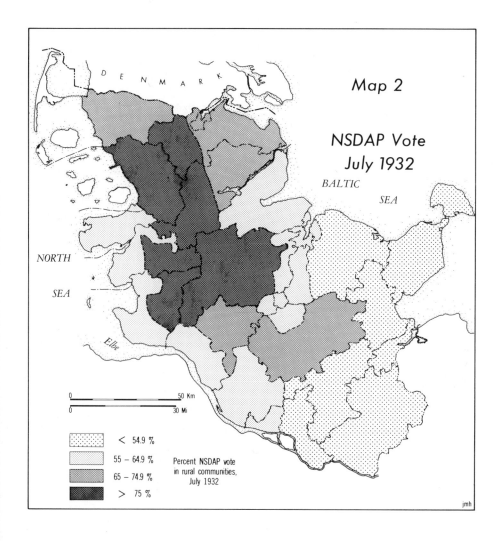

Map 2

NSDAP Vote
July 1932

Percent NSDAP vote
in rural communities,
July 1932

< 54.9 %
55 – 64.9 %
65 – 74.9 %
> 75 %

Table I-3

*Elections to the Reichstag in Schleswig-Holstein Communities
with under 2,000 Population (Rural Communities),
in selected Minor Civil Divisions (Kreise), by Major Subregions,
1919 to 1932*

Percentage of Total Vote

	NSDAP	Land-volk	DNVP	DVP	Landes-partei	DDP	Other Parties (non-Soc.)	SPD	USPD	KPD
Marsh										
1919	--	--	7.6	9.0	8.2	29.3	--	45.9	--	--
1921	--	--	29.0	20.1	5.0	6.4	0.1	27.6	6.4	5.4
1924 I	6.4	--	40.6	10.4	--	9.3	5.8	19.0	1.3	7.2
1924 II	3.1	--	41.4	11.5	--	11.5	3.4	24.7	--	4.4
1928	7.9	0.5	29.6	9.3	--	4.6	15.4	27.6	--	5.1
1930	41.2	7.0	5.3	3.1	--	2.8	6.8	25.5	--	8.3
1932 I	61.6	--	6.2	--	--	--	4.0	19.4	--	8.8
Geest										
1919	--	--	3.9	4.7	38.4	21.8	0.1	31.1	--	--
1921	--	--	25.3	13.0	27.5	5.7	0.9	22.1	3.5	2.0
1924 I	9.4	--	47.3	11.7	--	6.7	6.9	14.1	0.5	3.4
1924 II	2.4	--	49.9	18.1	--	8.6	3.3	16.1	--	1.6
1928	15.9	1.1	24.3	14.0	--	3.6	21.7	17.5	--	1.9
1930	45.9	14.2	3.7	3.7	--	3.0	11.6	14.7	--	3.2
1932 I	78.7	--	3.8	--	--	--	4.5	9.7	--	3.3

Table I-3 (continued)

Hill Zone										
1919	---	---	15.8	6.3	14.3	21.7	0.3	39.6	2.0	---
1921	---	---	28.2	15.6	6.2	7.8	0.4	34.6	4.9	2.3
1924 I	5.5	---	38.7	13.7	---	6.7	2.8	24.0	1.0	7.6
1924 II	1.9	---	40.9	15.7	---	6.9	2.0	29.2	---	3.4
1928	2.0	0.4	32.7	15.0	---	4.3	10.0	32.6	---	3.0
1930	24.3	10.4	10.9	6.1	---	5.2	10.4	27.8	---	4.9
1932	57.1	---	10.0	---	---	---	4.9	21.4	---	6.6

Marsh = *Eiderstedt*, North and South Dithmarschen.
Geest = Kreis Rendsburg, Flensburg, Schleswig, North and South Dithmarschen.
Hill Zone = Flensburg, Schleswig, *Eckernförde, Plön, Oldenburg, Landesteil Lübeck* (of freestate of Oldenburg).
The italicized civil divisions are as a whole apportioned to the subregion, the others in part.
Some communities on the edge of marsh and Geest and in the marshes along the Eider River have been disregarded.

Source: Heberle, *From Democracy to Nazism*, p. 99.

graphical areas, beginning each analysis with a
sketch of the economic and social structure peculiar
to the area.

   A. *The west coast marshes* extend from the Elbe
north into Denmark; this thin stretch of land comprises only 14 percent of the total area of
Schleswig-Holstein, but its soils are among the most
fertile.[21] These rich soils, colonized and reclaimed
from the sea by settlers from the southern Geest and
by Frisians and Dutch, fostered a breed of wealthy,
proud, and independent farmers. The *Dithmarscher* in
particular have a reputation for being *dickköpfig*
(obstinate); government officials often find them a
trying folk. Their pronounced independence has its
origins in the history of this area. The farmers of
Dithmarschen and Eiderstedt never fell into serfdom;
in a series of still-celebrated battles they managed
to preserve the ancient liberties of German free-
holders and to retain all the essential features of
self-government until Prussia gained control of
Schleswig-Holstein. Before Prussian rule the most
affluent farmers exercised authority and ran local
affairs so as to promote their own interests.
   The nature of the marsh economy allowed these
wealthy farmers time for politics, for commercial
and speculative pursuits, and for boisterous enter-
tainments. From the nineteenth century onward they
began to specialize in raising beef cattle, first
for English and then for more distant domestic
markets. They bought young cattle from Geest
farmers in the spring, fattened them on the lush
marsh grass, and sold them in the fall; since cattle-
grazing does not impose heavy regular work, the
large farmer was politically available. Wheat and
cabbage were other important crops; the area around
Wesselburen is today still the most important
cabbage-producing center of West Germany, and Marne
the focus of a second important cabbage region.
Both cattle and cabbage were highly speculative
crops. Profits in the cattle business depended upon
being able to buy cheaply in the spring and sell at
a profit in the fall; the cabbage market fluctuated
wildly depending on the success of the crop. Small
fortunes could be made in both crops, but the risk
accompanying heavy dependence on market conditions
was large. A high element of risk continues to
characterize the present-day agriculture of the
marshes.

The class structure of the marshes channeled
the area's wealth into the hands of the possessors,
and the society of the area, especially in Dithmarschen, reflected these sharp class differences:

> It lacked informal daily contact, especially
> among the women; it lacked the common play of
> children on the village street, and even on
> family holidays and other occasions on which
> the whole Geest village came together, the
> marsh farmers remained aloof. Marriages
> between farm families and their hired help
> virtually did not exist, while in the diversely-
> stratified villages the possibility of gradual
> social mobility through marrying into the next
> higher layer of society was greater.[22]

The settlement pattern perpetuated class barriers.
Individual farmers and workers might maintain
amiable relations, but real community between the
two classes was impossible:

> The deep cleavage between rich and poor,
> between farmer and cottager or laborer, is
> emphasized by the settlement pattern: the
> farmers live on single farmsteads with spacious
> buildings in the midst of the fields and pas-
> tures; the poor, the working-class people, live
> in villages and in small line-settlements along
> the sea dikes and the edge of the Geest.[23]

The organization of labor cemented these divisions:
the large farms were operated with comparatively few
workers recruited from among the poor. The largest
farmers could avoid manual labor altogether, but
even the next stratum, who did do farm work themselves, lived and conducted themselves like gentle-
men. The younger sons of these wealthy farmers
sought their fortunes in Hamburg, and thus the marsh
elite came to be related by kinship and marriage
with the professions, the clergy, and the civil
service. A military tradition was not lacking;
"even before the First World War the men often held
commissions in the army reserve."[24]
    Before 1918 the rich marsh farmers adhered to
the National Liberal or Free Conservative parties;
the smaller farmers, the small-town middle class,
and the working class gave their allegiance to the
Progressives. Following the revolution the SPD

built up its organization in rural areas it had
previously been unable to penetrate; the SPD organ,
the *Schleswig-Holsteinische Volkszeitung*, reported
on July 12, 1919:

> Particularly gratifying is the fact that in the
> "black corner" of the district, the west coast
> of Schleswig, organizing also proceeds apace.
> In the former fourth electoral district
> [Tondern-Husum] alone the number of local orga-
> nizations has climbed from 6 to 19 and the
> number of members from 119 to 2,379.[25]

Doubtless some of these new units and members came
from Geest areas, but the Marxist parties clearly
had powerful new support in the marsh. In rural
Eiderstedt and Dithmarschen the SPD polled 45.9
percent of the vote in 1919. Even larger farmers
reportedly voted SPD, not because they supported the
party's goals, but because they wanted to protest
against those social classes they thought responsible
for the war and its outcome.[26] The DDP obtained
29.3, and no party of a more conservative stripe
received as much as 10 percent of the vote.
    The Left (SPD, USPD, and KPD) maintained its
strength in the marshes at a fairly consistent
level from 1920 on (see Table I-3). The Liberals,
however, suffered a catastrophic decline from 38.8
percent of the vote in 1919 (46.5 percent if one
includes the *Landespartei*) to virtual extinction in
1932. The Conservatives (DNVP) at first reaped the
benefits of the Liberals' decline, but their following soon defected to the Nazis. Of the causes of
this turn to the NSDAP in the marshes Heberle
states, "An explanation may be attempted in terms of
increasing economic insecurity rather than of actual
suffering from the agricultural depression."[27] The
lower selling prices and tighter credit of the late
twenties hit the high-risk agriculture of the
marshes especially hard. Near the Elbe the decline
of horse breeding (because of motorization and the
reduction of army demands) and the crisis in such
local rural industries as basket making compounded
the effects of repeated crises in the important hog-
raising sector and served to arouse discontent with
the existing political system and to create support
for the Nazis. This insecurity of living standards
Heberle regards as the chief cause of the turn to
Nazism in the marsh region.

Table I-4

Radicalization of "Middle Class" Parties
in Rural Communities of Dithmarschen
by Subregions

	Percentage of Total Vote Cast for Middle-Class Parties		Percentage of Middle-Class Party Votes Cast for NSDAP	
	Marsh	*Geest*	*Marsh*	*Geest*
1924 I	69.4	84.9	10.2	7.0
1924 II	68.7	85.8	5.5	3.6
1928	63.3	82.4	16.1	41.1
1930	63.6	82.0	66.5	67.4
1932	69.0	87.7	87.1	92.1

Source: Heberle, *From Democracy to Nazism*,
         p. 103.

From 1928 the Nazis never achieved the same
high percentage of success in the marshes that they
did on the Geest, primarily because of the larger
and more stable Socialist vote in the marshes. The
rural working class of the marshes posed an obstacle
to Nazi penetration that the less numerous and less
class-conscious rural proletariat of the Geest did
not. Heberle properly observes this point, but then
proceeds to make a more questionable argument; he
claims that "the *proportion* of the total vote for
the non-Marxist or 'middle class' parties [this
designation apparently includes the DNVP] which went
to the Nazis was on the whole smaller in the marshes
of Dithmarschen than on the Geest, although in some
earlier elections the relation had been the
reverse."[28]
     In support of this contention, Heberle produces
the data in Table I-4; however, the table shows only
that in the marshes a higher proportion of middle-
class voters remained with the traditional middle-
class parties somewhat longer. The *rapidity* of Nazi
gains among voters for middle-class parties on the
Dithmarscher Geest from 1924 to 1928 strikes one
more forcefully than the eventual differences in
proportions. The differences in the *tempo* of the

formation of new allegiances (i.e., the longer
resistance in the marshes to massive inroads by the
Nazis) cannot be explained by economic factors,
Heberle argues; rather the greater stability of
political loyalties

> probably rests above all upon the greater
> stability of political tradition among the
> marsh farmers; they were the well-off, the
> more businesslike, the better educated; they
> provided the leading political families;
> accordingly certain political attitudes had
> engrained themselves that were harder for a
> new (and to the possessors of great property,
> socially inferior) movement to shake.[29]

Of this entire analysis I shall have more to say
later.[30]

  B. *The eastern hill area* extends over 41
percent of the surface area of Schleswig-Holstein
and contains the most fertile soils. It includes
three distinct subregions: (1) the district of
large estates in Eckernförde, Plön, and Oldenburg;
(2) the farmers' districts of the Probstei (the
northwest corner of *Kreis* Plön) and Angeln; and (3)
the Isle of Fehmarn. The entire region's agriculture is well diversified except in Fehmarn, where
the economy rests heavily on grain. Fehmarn forms
in social terms an intermediate stage between the
family farm and large estate areas. The class
structure and social conditions here resemble those
prevailing in Dithmarschen and the political evolution of the island has been similar.
  The area of large estates (*Güter*) in East
Holstein endured nearly feudal conditions until the
early twentieth century.[31] These large manors
resembled the East Elbean estates, with the difference that the large landowners of East Holstein had
not been able to subject their area to quite the
same degree of control as their East Elbean counterparts. They did have the same control over government and in prewar days they had not hesitated to
fire workers who voted Social Democratic, or even to
seize SPD ballots,[32] but their serfs had been freed
a century before those in Prussia and a class of
quite well-to-do tenant farmers emerged, most of
whom had held the same farm for generations either
as *Zeitpaechter* (long-term tenants) or *Erbpaechter*

(hereditary tenants). Throughout the region these tenant farm holdings were mixed with the estates, the tenants with the cottagers and day-laborers of the large manors. After 1919 these tenants gained possession of their land, but often at prices the smaller tenants could not afford. The Communists made inroads among this group of precarious smallholders by attacking the banks' rigid foreclosure policies.

The Probstei consisted of farmers who had lived free of seigneurial rule and domination for over a century. They employed more modern technological methods on their farms and enjoyed a comparatively high standard of living. They lived in closely knit communities with minimal class divisions. Angeln displayed a well-diversified economy and a more complicated social structure. Here a small group of estate owners shared the pleasures of ruling with a class of large farmers. Beneath these strata came a substantial body of smaller farmers and cottagers, and at the bottom a class of day laborers and hired hands. The landless workers had some opportunity for moving into the class of cottagers. Labor relations retained a tinge of patriarchalism and there was considerable social intercourse among the various classes.

> On the whole what presents itself is the picture of a peasant society with fewer social tensions than in Dithmarschen or Fehmarn, in which despite a clearly developed "class" stratification the differences in class situation had not led to the formation of sharp class contradictions and conflicts.[33]

The quality of the soil and the well-diversified rural economy favored this gradual stratification; the good soil permitted a family to nourish itself from a relatively small plot, and the varied branches of production provided a demand for labor throughout the year.

The political traditions of the estate areas and the family farm areas differed as much as their social structures. The large estate owners had a long conservative tradition; in the 1920s they supported the DNVP, although they no longer dominated this party as they had its prewar predecessors. The agricultural laborers, small farmers, and tenants gave their sympathies to the Democratic and

Socialist parties and, following the revolution of
1918, these parties won large majorities in the
estate districts. Angeln had a quite different
tradition. Here the upper classes were not so
conservative as in East Holstein. In 1919 the
Landespartei, with strong roots in Angeln, emerged
as the largest party with 35.5 percent of the vote;
the DDP obtained 27.9 percent, and the DVP 8 percent. The socialist parties formed a small but
relatively firm block.

In general the DNVP and the socialist parties
had their best success in the sharply-divided class
society of the estate regions; the liberal parties
and the Nazis dominated the farmer's districts,
although here too the DNVP enjoyed a period of
ascendancy in the middle twenties. Heberle has
compiled a table showing the striking differences
(see Table I-5). In the estate areas the long
tradition of class solidarity and class conflict
checked Nazi advances, but in the organic communities of Angeln the NSDAP won 70.8 percent of the
vote in July 1932.

C. *The Geest's* poor sandy soils and moors
cover roughly 45 percent of Schleswig-Holstein. Not
until the end of the nineteenth century did the use
of artificial fertilizer and other technical improvements begin to dispel the poverty of this area. Even
then the simple standards of the region continued,
and into the 1920s the Geest farmer could be identified by his black peasant blouse. The Geest was
quite simply a backward rural region:

> Sparse settlement, particularly on the poorer,
> eastern part of the Geest; remoteness from
> urban centers, above all in Schleswig, which
> was relatively isolated from transport facili-
> ties; little tourism in comparison with the
> lake-covered hill country and the North Sea
> coast—all no doubt contributed to preserving
> the Geest from urbanization and its population
> from urbanity.[34]

Small wonder that the wealthy marsh farmers dismissed
the Geest farmers with a contemptuous or conde-
scending *"man 'n lütten Geestbuer"*—"just a little
Geest farmer!"

On the sparse Geest soils the farmers planted
rye, a less valuable crop than the wheat and barley

Table I-5

Election Results in Rural Communities in the Eastern Hill Zone

Type of Community	NSDAP		DNVP		SPD and KPD	
	1932	*1930*	*1932*	*1930*	*1932*	*1930*
Estates prevalent						
Kreis Oldenburg	41.4	16.0	11.0	18.6	45.0	49.6
Kreis Ploen	45.3	18.8	9.8	15.3	42.4	46.5
Farmers' villages						
Isle of Fehmarn	47.0	23.9	8.6	16.7	41.8	44.3
Kreis Oldenburg	52.0	25.5	9.3	19.0	36.4	41.6
Kreis Ploen	52.2	23.9	10.9	16.7	33.9	36.1
Probstei	59.5	38.0	11.8	17.4	26.0	29.7
Kreis Eckernfoerde (mixed)	60.1	22.2	9.2	11.3	28.2	31.4
Angeln (Farmers)	70.8	24.6	10.5	7.0	12.5	15.0

Source: Heberle, *From Democracy to Nazism,* p. 107.

grown in Dithmarschen and East Holstein. They concentrated on cattle breeding, and although chickens
and dairying provided a steadier stream of income
and reduced the need for seasonal credits well below
marsh levels, the Geest farmer's ultimate dependence
upon the price of beef left him in a more precarious
situation than the eastern hill area farmers. The
Schleswig Geest farmer in particular felt this
dependence; farther south the large urban centers
encouraged milk production and truck farming and
thus provided separate sources of income.

Middle and small farmers determined the social
structure of the Geest. Only a very few large
estates existed on the Geest, and rather than a
large class of agricultural laborers one found hired
hands who lived in the same village with their
employers, worked in the fields with them, and
socialized together.

> The separation of *Gut* and *Dorf* (estate and vil-
> lage), which in the eastern zone symbolizes the
> class structure, and the isolation of the big
> farmers on their scattered homesteads, which is
> characteristic of the marsh, are not found here;
> the Geest is a region of peasant villages. The
> Geest farmer has caught less of the spirit of
> capitalistic enterprise than the marsh farmer;
> he is in mentality and in habits still more of
> a peasant...class distinctions are scarcely
> noticeable, and a spirit of neighborliness and
> true community prevails.[35]

Here one spoke of *Dorfgemeinschaft* (village community). In this society no ruling class above the
local level developed; even the prosperous Geest
farmers failed to develop a political tradition or
to participate strongly in rural interest group
organizations before 1918. Heberle suggests that
this lack of political leadership, combined with
community solidarity, accounts for the great swings
of political opinion in this region. He adds that
the lack of a strong socialist bloc offered the
Nazis a larger reservoir of potential voters.

This last factor was decisive. Except for a
few working-class communities around larger cities
and the rural workers on the western edge of the
Geest, the socialist parties had few adherents. The
Geest population gave its vote to anti-Marxist parties, first to the *Landespartei* and the DDP, then in

the middle twenties to the DNVP, and then finally
and overwhelmingly to the NSDAP. The essential
difference between the Geest and the other two rural
regions was that in the marsh and the hill district
the rural working class voted steadily and dominantly
for one of the socialist parties, whereas on the
Geest the less numerous rural proletariat shed its
early allegiance to the SPD to vote in considerable
degree first DNVP and then for the Hitler movement.

> On the whole, the difference in the radicaliza-
> tion of non-socialist voters in marsh and Geest
> was not very significant in contrast to the
> hill land, where a larger percentage of "bour-
> geois" voters held out against the NSDAP. If
> the NSDAP obtained a higher collective per-
> centage of votes in 1930 and 1932 on the Geest
> than in the marsh, that result can be traced
> above all to the weakness of the socialist
> parties on the Geest.[36]

The analysis strongly suggests that the predominance
of middle-class family farmers and the absence of a
distinct "upper" and especially of a "lower" class
explains the greater susceptibility of the Geest
population to Nazism.[37]

Having concluded his regional analysis of
voting patterns, Heberle proceeds to reinforce his
findings with a series of correlations between party
strength and socioeconomic factors. The assumption
behind such analysis is, of course, that a party
based on a certain social class will receive a percentage of the vote in proportion to the percentage
of this class in a given area. In the first set of
correlations, Heberle shows the relationship between
voting patterns in rural areas and the percentage of
those employed in agriculture on farms of varying
size (see Table I-6). Heberle uses the percentages
of those employed in agriculture rather than the
percentages of all farms in the specified sizes,
because the former indicator has a closer relation
to the number of voters. He combines farms under
two hectares (about 5 acres) with those over one
hundred (about 250 acres) because the small farms
generally represented plots of tenants and cottagers
who worked on large estates.
The data in the table confirm Heberle's analysis of the relationships between class structure

Table I-6

Schleswig-Holstein: Correlations between Percentages of Total Valid Vote Obtained in Rural Communities of 18 Minor Civil Divisions, and Percentages of all Gainfully Employed Workers in Agriculture** on Farms of Specified Size

Parties and Years of election		Farm Size Classes		
		Small Farms—2-20 hectares (Kleinbauern)	Large Farms—20-100 hectares (Grossbauern)	Estates and Very Small Farms—100 or more and Less than 2 hectares
Socialists SPD, USPD, KPD	1919	−.97	−.43	+.88
	1921	−.98	−.45	+.95
	1930	−.92	−.43	+.92
	1932	−.80	−.40	+.83
Democrats and Landespartei	1919	+.89	+.52	−.94
	1921	+.80	+.34	−.77
Conservatives DNVP	1919	−.70	−.34	+.76
	1921	−.19	−.04	+.02
	1930	−.60	−.49	+.61
	1932	−.80	−.40	+.83
Landvolk	1930	+.59	+.26	−.64
NSDAP & Landvolk	1930	+.79	+.45	−.82
NSDAP	1930	+.43	+.26	−.43
	1932	+.85	+.49	−.89

*   Province of Schleswig-Holstein and part of Oldenburg.

** *Landwirtschaftliche Erwerbstätige.*

Source: Heberle, *From Democracy to Nazism*, p. 114.

and election results. The Conservative party and
socialist parties did best in those areas where
large percentages of workers were employed on large
estates; the correlation between strong socialist
voting and the prevalence of estates and very small
farms ranges from +.83 to +.95. The Nazis fared
best in areas with small and medium-sized farms; the
correlation between Nazi balloting in 1932 and the
presence of small farmers (*Kleinbauern*) is a remarkable +.85. Equally eye-catching is the high negative correlation (-.89) between Nazi support and
estate areas.

A second set of correlations (see Table I-7)
gives a more extensive view. Table I-7 requires
some explanation. German statistics distinguish
between (1) *Erwerbspersonen*, persons in gainful
occupations, including the unemployed, and (2)
Berufszugehörige, persons dependent on a certain
occupation or industry (i.e., *Erwerbspersonen* plus
their dependents). Heberle employs the latter category since he is interested in the behavior of all
voters, not just those in a gainful occupation. The
statistics also distinguish among the following
"classes": (a) *Selbständige*, owners and proprietors; (b) *Beamten und Angestellten*, officials and
salaried employees; (c) *Arbeiter*, workers or wage
earners, and (d) *Mithelfende Familienangehörige*,
family members employed in the business or on the
farm of the head of the household (this last category is a useful indicator of the petty bourgeois
stratum). These categories cannot be equated with
social classes, because they contain quite different
social groups. The category *Selbständige* includes
the owners of vast estates as well as small farmers,
wealthy factory owners in addition to impecunious
shopowners. These categories are, however, the best
available and they provide a rough measure of social
structure—e.g., the higher the percentage of
Selbständige and *Mithelfende Familienangehörige*, the
more pronounced the lower middle class character of
the area.

The data once again show the middle classes
voting first for the liberal parties, then for the
conservatives, and finally for the Nazis. The
correlation of the percentage of wage earners with
the socialist parties remains fairly constant or
even increases. Heberle concludes that this correlation "indicates that on the whole labor must have
adhered to the socialist parties,"[38] but it would

Table I-7

Schleswig-Holstein: Correlations between Percentages of Votes Obtained by Parties in 18 Minor Civil Divisions (cities of 10,000 or more population excluded) with Percentages of Population in Specified Socioeconomic Classes (Berufszugehörige) by Major Industrial Divisions

Party	Year	Agriculture, Forestry, Fishery			Industry, Handicraft		Industry, Commerce, Transportation		All Industrial Divisions including Public Services, Domestic Service, etc.	
		Proprietors (a)	a+m	Wage earners (c)	a	c	a	c	a	c
Socialists SPD, USPD, KPD	1921	−.84	−.88	+.86	−.68	+.65	−.70	+.62	−.93	+.95
	1932	−.79	−.78	+.77	−.84	+.82	−.81	+.69	−.94	+.88
Liberals DVP, DDP, Landespartei, and Center	1921	+.81	+.85	−.77	+.50	−.48	+.54	−.53	+.84	−.86
Conservatives	1921	−.20	±0.0	+.22	+.23	−.24	+.15	−.31	+.08	+.07
DNVP	1924 II	+.40	+.45	−.41	+.68	−.66	+.57	−.71	+.52	−.47
	1932 I	−.26	−.28	+.31	+.09	−.08	+.09	−.15	+.02	+.12
Landvolk	1930	+.67	+.69	−.64	+.58	−.30	+.49	−.39	+.74	−.77
NSDAP	1930	+.37	+.43	−.43	+.32	−.39	+.24	−.40	+.36	−.38
	1932 I	+.76	+.79	−.78	+.71	−.69	+.63	−.53	+.83	−.79

Explanation of occupational classifications:
a = proprietors; m = family members employed on farm; c = wage earners

Source: Heberle, *From Democracy to Nazism*, p. 118.

have been more judicious to conclude that these
figures show that the socialist parties continued to
receive the bulk of their support from the working
class—quite a different point. The high negative
correlation between the proportion of agricultural
workers and Nazi voting (-.78 in July 1932) does
imply, however, that the Nazis did not do well among
rural workers.

On the basis of the ecological analysis and the
correlations between electoral results and social
categories one can agree with Heberle that the rural
middle class of small farmers and entrepreneurs,
often celebrated as the sturdy foundation of a
stable democracy, proved the most susceptible to the
National Socialist movement, while the agricultural
and industrial workers resisted to a greater degree
the inroads of Hitlerism. The estate owners and big
farmers retained in large measure their adherence to
the DNVP, but one can interpret this loyalty in
different ways. Heberle chooses to characterize
them as "resistant"[39] to Nazism, and there is some
evidence to suggest that a vote for the DNVP was at
least partly a vote against the NSDAP; for example,
the DNVP Reichstag deputy, Dr. Oberfohren, the publisher of an important conservative newspaper in the
East Holstein estate area, actively opposed Nazism.[40]
As a whole, however, the DNVP after 1928 pursued a
program of reactionary subversion. The party in
Schleswig-Holstein supported this course. The
utterances of the DNVP Reichstag deputy, Max Soth
(Lockstedt), differed but little from those of the
Nazis. Here is the core of the problem of interpretation: given the counterrevolutionary program of
the DNVP and Hugenberg's cooperation with Hitler in
the Harzburg Front, ought one to emphasize the anti-
Nazi aspect of the DNVP vote, or is it preferable to
combine the DNVP and NSDAP ballots as the vote of
the radical anti-Marxist opposition to the Weimar
Republic? If one chooses the latter course, then
Heberle's material and conclusions look somewhat
different: the rural opposition to the Weimar
Republic is still more pronounced (73 percent versus
50 percent for urban areas—see Table I-2); the differences between the rural marsh and hill areas are
negligible (see Table I-3); and the estate owners
and big farmers share the responsibility for the
demise of the Republic more clearly.

This interpretation appears to be a useful
supplement to Heberle's conclusions, but the fact

that it can be made at all raises an important question of method. The electoral results do not have
such a clear and direct meaning as Heberle sometimes
implies—one must always interpret the significance
or meaning of a particular vote. A vote represents
a crude and drastic condensation of political opinion; votes for a given party may originate in the
most varied motives, from a highly rational investigation of different party programs and philosophies
to irrational personal inclination, from a shrewdly
calculated appraisal of class interest to physical
intimidation. From the voting figures alone one can
infer little about their objective significance
(their effect on the political system) and still less
about the subjective meaning (the voter's appraisal
of his choice).[41] Thus when Heberle speaks of "the
development of a political opportunism of fundamentally materialistic nature on the part of the middle
classes,"[42] he cannot base this assertion on his
study of electoral statistics, but only on his
personal observations; the statistics themselves do
not allow such a conclusion.

Since Heberle's path-breaking analysis, a
number of other scholars have extended and refined
his work. Gerhard Stoltenberg in his *Politische
Strömungen im schleswig-holsteinischen Landvolk*
(*Political Currents among the Rural Population of
Schleswig-Holstein*) relies largely upon the manuscript of Heberle's *Landbevölkerung und Nationalsozialismus* (*The Rural Population and National
Socialism*),[43] but expands this analysis in two
important ways. First, Stoltenberg describes
changes in the character of parties, their programs,
and their personnel. Here his discussion of the
DNVP has special importance.[44]

The DNVP began in 1919 with a declaration to
the tradition of the Reich, the German nation, and
property. Sociologically it had expanded beyond
the narrow noble clique of pre-1914 days to embrace
sections of the urban and rural middle class;
regionally, the party was strongest in the former
conservative strongholds of East Holstein. Certain
elements within the party had already begun to
inveigh against democracy, democrats, foreigners,
and Jews, but on the whole the climate was not yet
propitious for such agitation. By 1921, however,
the DNVP had scored a notable breakthrough, particularly on the west coast. A constant nationalist
agitation, often propounded by representatives of

the extreme antirepublican right, brought the party
a steady stream of new converts and a stunning
success in the 1924 elections. Following the
December 1924 election, the party decided to try to
exert influence from within the government and
joined the new coalition. While this course encouraged some of its supporters to hope for an *evolu-
tionary* reconstruction of the state, others within
its ranks were disenchanted with the shift from
radical agitation to participation in the government. The DNVP's large losses in the 1928 elections
demonstrated that the party's new course had alien-
ated many of its former supporters, and shortly
after the elections the uncompromising opponents of
the Republic, led by Hugenberg, took control of the
party. From this point until after the July 1932
elections, the DNVP attacked the Weimar "system"
with nearly the same intensity as did the NSDAP, but
the party had exhausted most of its political capital through its participation in the government.

These changes in the character of the party, as
described by Stoltenberg, allow a deeper understand-
ing of the shifts in political opinion than Heberle's
static appraisal of the DNVP as a "conservative"
party. Stoltenberg indicates the party's minimal
support in the revolutionary period, but he also
shows how easily the DNVP gained support for its
counterrevolutionary program and how its participation in the government splintered its following.
His analysis suggests that the rural population's
turn from the democratic to the conservative parties
in the early 1920s was at least as decisive, and
perhaps even more abrupt, than the shift to the
Nazis in the late twenties so carefully documented
by Heberle.

The second important contribution by Stoltenberg
is his mention of elections below the national level.
He does not analyze these elections in detail, but
his is the credit for having introduced them into
the discussion.[45] One vital fact emerges from
Stoltenberg's remarks: the nonsocialist democratic
parties failed to strike roots at the local level.
As early as the local elections of 1919 this tendency was clearly evident; of 456 elected local
district representatives, 223 belonged to a multi-
tude of nonpartisan local bourgeois groupings.

The middle class and the farmers thoroughly
preferred to fight these communal elections as

predominantly local and economic contests,
waiting to come together in neutral, politically indifferent slates. This procedure con-
formed most closely to the ideas of the Right,
which already in the course of 1919 began
rising gradually to sharper tones of opposition.[46]

These tendencies increased in the following local
elections; the bourgeois parties yielded to local
"economic" groupings (*Wählergemeinschaften* or sometimes "*Rathausparteien*") who claimed to be above the
hassle of partisan politics. The democratic
parties' lack of local organization and the attacks
of these local electoral alliances on the party
system eased the way for the Nazis to bring about
a switch of political allegiances.

These local electoral alliances by no means
represented a solid bourgeois front. In numerous
regions the bourgeoisie split along economic lines:

> Especially among the economic interest organi-
> zations of the small towns and the countryside
> there arose sharp differences and personal
> defamation that clearly reflected the problem-
> atic status of the oft-cited notion of a "bour-
> geois" or "middle-class" spirit—or solidarity
> of interests.[47]

The political system favored this fragmentation into
tiny parties representing specific interests, for if
a particular group of interests could not entice a
party to accept its batch of candidates, these
interests could form a party of their own and under
the system of proportional representation be reason-
ably certain of winning seats. The resulting pro-
liferation of small "apolitical" parties reflected
the failure of the liberal democratic parties to
build an organization in rural areas. But more
important, the growth of minor parties was symptom-
atic of rural distrust, first, of those parties
which concentrated on the interests of the urban
middle class and presented largely urban candidates
in national elections, and, second, of the system of
parties and parliamentary representation as a whole.
In rural Schleswig-Holstein the conservative forces
declared their allegiance to Baron von Stein's doc-
trines of local government at the same time that
they were undermining the position of the democratic
political parties.

The most careful student of this development has been Peter Wulf.[48] Wulf points out that as early as 1921 farmers and craftsmen were acting to reduce or even exclude the national parties from local politics.

> The artisans (*Das Handwerk*) argued that the local assemblies did not have political, but practical managerial tasks to accomplish and that their activity did not belong to the larger political sphere: local elections were in their view "administration elections."[49]

In accordance with this conception of politics a peculiar kind of local corporatism developed, with interest groups usurping many of the traditional functions of political parties. The local elections of 1925 showed that the rural middle class no longer looked to the political parties for representation of its interests on the local or even on the provincial level. Wulf interprets this rejection of the parties in favor of pure interest representation as part of a process which hit a peak just before the economic crisis of the late twenties.

This process had two crucial aspects: voters detached themselves from the bourgeois parties, and they assembled in loose electoral alliances which the Nazis easily penetrated. In the local elections of 1929 the Nazis exploited both of these developments: individual members ran as candidates on bourgeois lists, and the party itself won over many of those who had formerly voted for the local alliances. "*The increase in National Socialist Kreistag seats in the 1929 local elections is to be explained less by the decline of the political parties than by the halving of the percentages of those half-political peasant and middle-class corporate interest slates.*"[50] In 1933, bourgeois lists appeared in opposition to the Nazis in local elections, but for the most part their character had changed; now they represented not middle-class economic interests, but the few respectable conservatives who remained.

Wulf's electoral analysis provides further evidence of the weak allegiance of the rural middle classes to the Weimar Republic. It corroborates the view developed here that the rural population of Schleswig-Holstein, particularly the farmers, craftsmen, and merchants, did not make an abrupt transition from a staunch liberalism to Nazism, but rather had never shown great enthusiasm for the

Weimar Republic. This point emerges, however, not from an analysis of the electoral results them- selves—these show only the susceptibility of the property-owning classes to Nazism—but from a more detailed analysis of the evolution of the "political atmosphere." The methodology of political ecology and statistical correlation has been valuable in identifying Nazi supporters and in suggesting their political development, but it cannot of itself expose the causes of this development; to understand the Nazification of the rural middle classes, it is necessary to engage in a more detailed political analysis.

2: The Social Origins of Nazism in Rural Schleswig-Holstein

When confronted with the problem of explaining the success of the Nazi movement in their region, the rural people of Schleswig-Holstein resort to a crude economic determinism. The massive Nazi majorities of the early 1930s, they maintain, resulted from the disastrous economic situation. In interview after interview respondents stressed the staggeringly high urban unemployment as the chief causal factor behind Hitler's triumph. Secondarily they lamented the fate of agricultural producers in the Weimar era. They interpreted the economic collapse not merely as a necessary condition for the Nazis' rise, but as a sufficient one. One almost never heard any indication that nationalistic attitudes and social prejudices had played a part. Fears of Communism and the rigors of the Versailles Treaty were the two "noneconomic" factors most often cited. This bad history, a mixture of fading memories and popular historical accounts, tells more about the state of contemporary politics than it does about the Nazi victory, for it ignores much of the most essential and most embarrassing aspects of Hitler's electoral triumphs.

Nonetheless this simplistic economic explanation of the rural response to Nazism flourishes not merely in popular imagination, but in more scholarly efforts as well. In an instructive and generally reliable piece of local history, Dr. Broder Christensen, the former business director of the *Kreisbauernverband Husum*, pays due obeisance to the late Weimar Republic's "approximately seven million unem-

ployed" and then carefully and in great detail
describes the economic misery in rural Husum between
1927 and 1933. He concludes his account with the
suggestion that the farmers' turn to the Nazis was
an understandable response to their deteriorating
economic position:

> In order to transmit to the young, upcoming
> farm generation a picture of this time of dis-
> tress I have described in the greatest possible
> detail this period of decline in the agricul-
> ture of our country and the struggle of the
> farmers for their existence that was neces-
> sarily connected with it. *At the same time I
> have hoped to awaken thereby an understanding
> that our farmers—seeking aid and deliver-
> ance—joined a political movement, the NSDAP,*
> that had as its program, not only rescuing the
> farmers, but creating a place for them in the
> state that corresponded to their importance in
> its economy and national life.[1] [My emphasis.]

In this account Christensen discounts the possible
impact of antiliberal and antidemocratic impulses
among the local peasantry. Such an interpretation
is not only historically inaccurate, but politically
dangerous as well, for it disguises important elements involved in the Nazis' successes and mislead-
ingly implies that the prevailing peasant attitudes
were harmless or even benign.
     This chapter refutes such exclusively economic
explanations of Nazism in rural Schleswig-Holstein.
In brief, the argument is that real economic hardship did exist, but that the correlation between
agricultural distress and adherence to Nazism was
far from perfect; furthermore, comparisons with the
effects of agricultural depression in Scandinavia,
where Fascism failed to gain a substantial following, demonstrate the implausibility of attributing
the rise of Nazism to the depression alone. Radical
reaction had taken root in Schleswig-Holstein well
before the onset of the depression. These forces
nurtured oppositionist sentiments among the rural
population through such agencies as the radical
Landvolk movement; their activities prepared the
ground well for an energetic and well-organized
movement like Nazism. Thus the social origins of
Nazism must be traced not merely to the precarious
economic situation of certain social classes, but

also to the attitudes which these classes held and
which prepared them to interpret their economic
experience in categories favorable to the Nazi
cause.

The agricultural depression was severe; on this
point the evidence speaks eloquently. In 1926 and
1928 Schleswig-Holstein led all other Prussian provinces in the number of forced auctions, and after
1928 the number rose sharply as table II-1 indicates. Over the entire period Dithmarschen with 110
forced sales and Schleswig with 75 were the two
areas most sharply hit; only Plön and East Holstein
remained relatively unscathed. The table actually
understates the seriousness of the situation,
because from 1928 the farmers organized to prevent
foreclosures; in *Kreis* Husum alone a farmers' emergency committee saved 143 farms from coming under
the hammer.[2]

Farm prices descended precipitously over the
same period. One price index for farm products
which registered 137.8 in 1927 dipped to 82.5 at the
beginning of 1933.[3] Not all prices declined at the
same time or at the same rate. In 1926-27, before
the general agricultural slump began, hog prices
went into a cyclical decline as foreign imports and
domestic overproduction glutted the Hamburg market.
In 1929-30 hog prices dropped again, this time
affecting not just the hog-raising centers in *Kreis*
Steinburg, but the entire Geest as well. But the
real crisis began in 1930-31 when cattle prices
began to fall, disrupting the cattle-breeding and
cattle-raising economies of the Geest and marsh. In
the spring of 1931 marsh farmers paid on the Husum
market 50 to 60 RM (Reichsmark) a hundredweight for
their lean cattle, a price which just barely compen-
sated the Geest farmers for raising them. In August
the marsh farmers could sell the fattened cattle for
only 41 RM per hundredweight; by November the price
sank to 31 RM per hundred pounds—for the best
cattle delivered at the market.[4] Milk and grain
prices held up a bit longer, but they too began to
fall.

The province's agricultural economy rested
largely upon those products for which demand was
most elastic, upon meat, milk, butter, and vegetables rather than upon grain, and thus the industrial
depression hit Schleswig-Holstein harder than other
areas. The urban consumers of the Ruhr, Saxony,
Berlin, Hamburg, Kiel, and Lübeck, the primary

Table II-1

Forced Auctions in Schleswig-Holstein 1923-1932

	1923	1924	1925	1926	1927	1928	1929	1930	1931	1932
Number	--	1	16	45	33	76	89	95	143	202
Area (in hectares)	--	8	210	919	1,232	1,390	1,913	3,458	3,144	4,267

Source: Heberle, Landbevölkerung und Nationalsozialismus, p. 125.

markets for Schleswig-Holstein's farmers, restricted
their food purchases to the most essential items;
bacon and beef, milk, eggs, and vegetables appeared
less often on city tables, driving demand and prices
for these products down still farther. Tariffs
afforded little help; higher duties on grain benefited the East Elbean estate owners, but raised
fodder costs to many Schleswig-Holstein producers.
With declines in prices came drops in income. If
one examines the bookkeeping results of 564 farms as
compiled by the *Landwirtschaftskammer*, the picture
is not merely one of decline (see Table II-2). Such
figures must be interpreted with caution because of
their narrow base and the intrinsic difficulties of
agricultural accounting; nevertheless, they tend to
confirm the picture of sharp declines in 1927-28 and
1930-31 and the existence of less severe conditions
in grain-growing East Holstein.

Still another indicator of the seriousness of
the agricultural depression (and one that the farmers of the time were very much aware of) is the
increase in farmers' indebtedness. Indebtedness, of
course, does not always constitute an index of deteriorating economic status; it may indicate a willingness to employ borrowed capital to expand productive capacity. A higher level of debt may be a sign
of entrepreneurial confidence rather than of economic
weakness, and in the years immediately following the
great inflation, increases in indebtedness among
Schleswig-Holstein's farmers may be so interpreted.
"In the years from 1925 to 1928 agriculture seem-
ingly prospered, a development which may be traced
to excessively high levels of borrowing."[5] From
late 1927 the farmers felt these debts as an
increasing and increasingly unwelcome burden. From
1928 the figures on indebtedness become unreliable,
but there can be no doubt that farmers went further
into debt, this time against their will.[6]

A final index of the depression is the growing
underemployment in rural areas. The phenomenon of
rural underemployment resists precise statistical
diagnosis, but the facts were clear to contemporary
observers. Farmers' sons, who had hoped for an
illustrious career as doctors, lawyers, or army
officers, had to remain on the farm; those who did
go to the cities faced sharp competition for jobs
and advancement. The flight from the farm, which
had proceeded rapidly from the latter third of the
nineteenth century until 1925, ceased in the late

Table II-2

Taxable Farm Income in RM per Hectare of Farmland

	1927/1928	1928/1929	1929/1930	1930/1931
Eastern Hill Area	+11.83	+53.37	+52.02	+21.35
Marshes	-12.62	+31.80	+27.35	+15.54
Geest	- 8.32	+30.13	+32.12	+ 7.00
Southern Geest	-11.66	+43.88	+44.50	+12.03
Schleswig-Holstein	- 2.88	+41.46	+41.15	+15.37

Source: Condensed from Heberle, *Landbevölkerung und National-sozialismus*, p. 129.

twenties and early thirties. At the same time,
older farmers became more reluctant to retire and
bequeath their farms to their sons. Having seen the
inflation decimate their own savings and reduce
already retired farmers to dependence upon public
support, they delayed their retirement to avoid the
ignominy of a poverty-stricken old age. Rural youth
thus faced diminishing opportunities, both in the
city and in the country; a stratum of frustrated,
underemployed young men began to pile up, men with
grievances and with time on their hands—potential
SA men.

> ...the man who instead of becoming a well-
> established lawyer or physician had to be
> content with a small practice as a dentist or
> the humble position of a milk inspector, felt
> elated when he could march through the streets
> of the county seat at the head of a troop of
> Brown Shirts and break up a Communist meeting.[7]

The growing, restless population of young men was
another tangible sign and result of the general
depression, but the depression alone did not "make"
them Nazis.

The general course of the agricultural depression correlates rather well with the spread of
Nazism. The crisis began in the hog-raising areas
of Pinneberg and Steinburg and on the Dithmarscher
Geest. From there it spread into the marshes and to
the Geest as, with the beginning of the industrial
depression, urban consumers could no longer afford
the more expensive foodstuffs. Last and least
affected were the more diversified farms in the
eastern hill area. In all regions, the highly
specialized farms (which were usually the ones most
dependent upon credit as well) suffered to a greater
degree.

The depression had a varying impact on different social classes as well as on different
regions. The large estate owners of East Holstein
might show sizable declines in profits on their farm
operations, but they had ways to shore up their
positions: releasing workers or replacing them with
machinery, selling off some acreage, or even cutting
expenditures on conspicuous consumption. The small
farmers had no equivalent margin of safety. They
suffered most under the burden of debt. They
survived by working themselves and their families

still harder and by denying themselves even basic
comforts. Unionized farm workers maintained wage
levels fairly well in the early stages of the slump,
but later they lost the gains of the prosperous
years. Those workers who had been let go lived on
small unemployment benefits; nonunion workers just
eked out a living as best they could.

The "fit" between the impact of the depression
and Nazi success is, however, far from perfect: on
a regional, class, or individual basis the connection is not clear and simple. Angeln, for example,
endured the agricultural crisis comparatively well;
here the slump struck in late 1932 with the fall of
milk and grain prices. Yet in July the Nazis had
already obtained one of their highest majorities in
rural Angeln—70.8 percent.[8] The rural working
class felt the privations as sharply as any other
group, yet they largely retained their allegiance
to the Social Democrats or turned to the Communists
rather than to the Nazis. And there is evidence to
suggest that numerous wealthy individuals who suffered little from the depression eagerly supported
the Nazi cause. Prussian undercover agents customarily reported a large number of impressive automobiles present at Nazi rallies; they listed license
numbers in an effort to identify sympathizers. Bodo
Uhse, the editor of the Nazi *Tageszeitung* who later
turned Communist, recalled an early visit to the
home of Hein Hansen, the Nazi leader resident in
Breitenfelde; the table was covered with fine white
linen and adorned with good china, silver tableware,
and sparkling crystal glasses. Other rebellious
farmers were "not exactly the poorest"; they "sat
like lords on proud and splendid estates."[9]

This evidence does not demonstrate that the
depression was unimportant; it merely demonstrates
that the depression alone cannot constitute a sufficient explanation of Nazism's success in Schleswig-
Holstein. Economic events do not lead to political
conclusions in a clear and rigid way; men interpret
the significance of these economic events in the
light of their experience and intellectual tradition. The results of comparative studies further
confirm the point that economic difficulties alone
do not provide a satisfactory explanation of the
origins of the Nazi dictatorship.

This is demonstrated by just a brief glance
over the border toward Denmark, where a stur-

dier state with a more continuous and coherent
political tradition was able to endure and
eventually to solve the economic and above all
the political problems associated with the
agricultural crisis of the 1920s and its psychological effects.[10]

Denmark, Norway, and Sweden—to take just three
examples—all experienced depressions in the same
period, but managed to preserve democratic governments.
    The agricultural crisis struck hard in Denmark
as in Germany, but unprotected by tariff barriers
like the German farmers, the Danes had been forced
to begin modernizing their agriculture half a
century earlier. In the late twenties they produced more efficiently, provided better products,
marketed more skillfully, and delivered more reliably
than did the Germans. Marquis Childs reported
enthusiastically on the Danes' accomplishments:

> Agriculture in Denmark prior to the depression
> achieved the highest level of prosperity and
> efficiency in the world by virtue of coopera-
> tion and the most thorough education in scien-
> tific farming. And Denmark was able to send
> her agricultural products abroad to compete
> successfully in a half dozen markets because
> the profit of the middleman and the processor
> was largely eliminated.[11]

When the agricultural crisis arrived, Danish farmers
were better prepared to meet it—except for those in
the newly-annexed region of North Schleswig.
    The Danish rural depression began at the end of
1925, caused in part by fluctuations of the Danish
crown (its increased value made Danish farm exports
more expensive for foreign purchasers) and in part
by the 1925 German tariff on agricultural products.
This slump proved temporary, and the world depression did not hit Danish farmers until late 1930.
The worst period came in the next two years. Both
of the depressions, that of 1925-26 and that of
1930-33, spawned Fascist movements. In 1925 a
remarkable eccentric named Cornelius Petersen organized the "Self-Administration Movement," an anti-
parliamentary movement of larger farmers which
sought to detach North Schleswig from both Danish
and German control and to establish a Frisian

farmers' republic. Petersen maintained ties with
Copenhagen Fascists and employed Mussolini's appeals
to win supporters. He engaged in brutal defamation
of the parliamentary system and its leaders, and he
talked of a putsch, but he never got as far as even
a Danish version of the Munich Beer Hall fiasco. He
stood as a candidate in the 1926 elections, but
mustered only 2,117 votes out of a total of 66,843,
a defeat that effectively marked the end of his
movement. His fantastic ideas and his lack of
concern for the small farmer doomed him to defeat;
what antipathy to the Danish government he aroused
redounded largely to the benefit of the German party
in North Schleswig.[12] After its collapse Petersen's
movement was absorbed into a similar organization,
but one dominated by German irredentists with H. C.
Lei at their head. This movement foundered as
economic recovery in 1928 and 1929 stilled discontent.

     A nationwide Fascist threat did not emerge
until the early 1930s. Then an association named
Landbrugernes Sammenslutning (customarily called
simply LS) challenged the old liberal farm organizations and began employing syndicalist tactics to
obtain its ends. The LS contained two wings, of
which one was clearly Fascist, but the Fascists
never succeeded in gaining control of the movement
and the government's adept handling of the economic
crisis undercut the Fascists' efforts. Already in
1931 and 1932 the government had passed various laws
alleviating the pressure of indebtedness and providing financial aid to the most severely affected
farmers. In January 1933, the Danish Social Democrats and the Venstre Party (a liberal farmers'
party), drawn together by the depression, concluded
the compromise known as the *Kanslergadevergleich*,
devaluing the currency and thus stimulating agricultural exports. A special law for North Schleswig
and a trade treaty with England further improved
farmers' prospects, and the worst was over. The
Germans in North Schleswig eventually went over to
the Nazis, but the agreement between the representatives of farmers and of the urban workers succeeded
in quashing the growth of a native Danish Fascist
movement.[13]

     In Sweden and Norway farmers were similarly
enlisted for progressive reforms. In Sweden the
Social Democrats struck a bargain with the Farmers'
party in 1933; the Farmers' party agreed to support

the Social Democrats' program of public works in
exchange for further support for agriculture.[14]
Furthermore,

> In Norway (and in Sweden) the Social Democratic
> party succeeded in extending its influence
> among a considerable portion of the middle
> class—not least in rural areas—at the same
> time that its great German sister-party stood
> powerless before the spreading torrent of
> Nazism.[15]

In Norway the Quisling movement and a debtors' movement, known as the *Bygdefolkets Krisehjelp*, won the
support of some indebted farmers, but the failure of
Fascism in Norway "stands in sharp contrast to the
success of German Nazism, although the social and
economic conditions in several German provinces were
not dissimilar to those in Norway. This holds e.g.
for Schleswig-Holstein."[16]
      In 1933 the Fascists received 29 percent of the
vote in one part of the province of Telemark, but
only 2 percent in the country as a whole. The
Norwegian scholar Sten Nilson traces the contrasting
fates of German and Norwegian Fascism to a variety
of factors. First, Norway had very few large farms,
and about 75 percent of the small farmers had jobs
outside agriculture in the fishing, construction, or
timber industries. A sharp distinction between
farmers and workers simply did not exist, since many
workers owned a piece of land and many farmers
engaged—at least temporarily—in nonagricultural
employment.

> The word "Worker-Farmer" (*Arbeiterbauer*) that
> was often employed in the propaganda of the
> Norwegian workers' party contained a great deal
> of truth. A large part of the rural population
> considered themselves as being simultaneously
> farmers and workers, a circumstance which
> surely facilitated the spread of socialist
> influence in rural areas.[17]

Here was a clear distinction from Schleswig-Holstein,
where the SPD got votes among rural workers but not
from small farmers.
      A second important difference that Nilson per-
ceives is the Norwegian Socialists' greater interest
in agricultural problems. He attributes this dif-

ference to the fact that Norway industrialized
later, and thus its Social Democratic leaders were
often sons of farmers and men who took a real
interest in farmers' problems. The German Socialist
leaders, he claims, as sons of workers, worried only
about supplying food for the cities—when they
thought about agriculture at all. Nilson neglects
the SPD's belated effort in developing and adopting
an agricultural program (passed in Kiel in 1928 and
promoted largely by a professor at Kiel), but this
omission is perhaps justifiable, since the program
remained a scrap of paper; the SPD's new agricultural program swayed neither the farmers nor its own
cadres. And this point is really the decisive one:
the Norwegian Socialists interested themselves in
the small farmers and suggested proposals to alle-
viate their indebtedness, while the German Socialists tended to group small farmers and estate owners
and to write both off as members of the propertied
class.

A third essential distinction between the
Norwegian and German cases concerns the Norwegian
authorities' handling of foreclosures. Public
authorities acted with restraint; in one case they
arranged terms when the *Bygdefolket* group sought to
prevent a forced sale. When forced sales did occur,
they seldom meant that the farmer had to leave the
farm.

> Ordinarily the creditor had to buy the farm and
> in most cases he gave it back to the former
> owner or his son or another member of the
> family at a reduced price. Often the owner
> bought the farm himself at the auction on terms
> that made it possible for him to pay off his
> obligation in the future. Thus while the
> demands of the *Bygdefolket* and others for a
> legal reduction of all indebtedness were
> rejected, there occurred a *de facto* reduction
> in the majority of individual cases.[18]

Public banks could facilitate such arrangements.
Small private rural banks could not; when they felt
the financial pinch of the depression, they usually
had to squeeze their borrowers. Nonetheless, the
procedure of the public banks permitted a more
generous and humane treatment of the problem of
indebtedness than occurred in Schleswig-Holstein.

In Denmark, in Sweden, and in Norway, then, the
depression evoked responses quite different from

that in Germany. Social Democrats displayed greater
concern for the farmers' problems and a greater
capacity to handle them; but above all, the rural
population, schooled in a more democratic tradition,
largely rejected Fascist analyses of the crisis.
What was decisive in all three cases was not the
severity of the depression, but the rural people's
reaction to it, their interpretation of its causes,
and their choice of remedies. This conclusion
further confirms the inadequacy of the popular
explanation of Nazism as the result of the depression alone and directs attention to the attitudes
and propaganda which shaped the rural Schleswig-
Holsteiner's perception of the depression. Barrington
Moore, Jr., has sketched the nature of the problem
nicely:

> The partial failure of a set of institu-
> tions to live up to what is expected of them
> provides an atmosphere receptive to demands for
> a more or less extensive overhaul of the status
> quo. At this juncture the future course of
> events depends heavily upon the models of a
> better world that become available to various
> strategic groups in the population.[19]

How then did the rural people of Schleswig-Holstein
come to interpret the depression? What traditions
and what new models caused them to misperceive the
nature of the crisis? How did the Nazis manage to
enlist them?

The demands raised during the massive demonstrations of January 28, 1928, provide some indication of the state of mind of the rural population.
The impetus to these demonstrations came from a
rural notable, Otto Johannsen of Büsum. He issued a
call to the entire rural population and to the urban
middle class to gather and present their grievances
and to demand the unification of the agricultural
interest organizations; within the space of three
weeks, without any kind of formal organization,
Johannsen's proposal penetrated to the most distant
corners of rural Schleswig-Holstein. On the
appointed day approximately 140,000 people turned
out for mass rallies in twenty different cities.
They came in cars, horse-drawn farm wagons, on bicy-
cles, and by foot.

In Heide Johannsen himself spoke to about
20,000 people at the largest of the meetings.

Johannsen violently attacked the government
with the arguments of the patriotic (*völkischen*)
organizations. These organizations had also
clearly influenced the formulations in his ten-
point program. Among other things the program
demanded a completely new orientation of German
trade policy with "independence from foreign
sources of food" (*Nahrungsmittelfreiheit vom
Ausland*) as its aim, the prohibition of all
nonessential imports of agricultural products,
the immediate take-over by the state of mort-
gage interest payments, drastic measures to
lower the rate of interest, reduction of
"limitless" public expenditures, adjustment of
social outlays to the economic situation, immediate governmental disavowal of Germany's
unique war guilt, and moves to revise the
unbearable reparations burdens that were
reducing the German people to a slave-people.[20]

Johannsen, whose brother was the leader of the
vicious *Stahlhelm Westküste*, an organization which
had split from the Stahlhelm because the parent
organization was too mild, delivered only one of the
day's inflammatory speeches. In Meldorf two NSDAP
members spoke; in Flensburg at least one speaker
called for reunification with North Schleswig.

Elsewhere the demands remained more exclusively
economic. The Schleswig meeting urged stiffer
controls on government expenditures at all levels,
a reorganization of the tax structure, a reduction
of interest rates, and changes in trade policy
aiming at agricultural autarchy.[21] Here there was a
strong emphasis on the unity of the entire rural
population, farmers, workers, shopkeepers, and
craftsmen, and on the farmers' cause as the cause of
the entire population—both themes the Nazis would
later exploit. In the meeting at Husum similar
motifs appeared: the same dissatisfaction with the
state's monetary, trade, and fiscal policies.

The Husum gathering of 8,000 heard a good analysis of the causes of their problems, delivered by
the chief organizer of the demonstration, Heinrich
Reese of Süderhöft. The local newspaper reported
Reese's diagnosis of the situation:

After the flood of paper marks [inflation] and
the introduction of a stable currency in 1923-
24, the farmers lacked capital. Consequently

they had to assume debts upon debts at an
enormous rate of interest. The year 1925
brought no improvement; in 1926 hoof-and-mouth
disease aggravated the condition of our agriculture still more; 1927 was a devastating
rain-year, and today our agriculture faces
ruin....[22]

Given these conditions, the farmers felt perfectly
justified in asking state aid. Lowering interest
rates was entirely possible, another Husum speaker
argued; the state had done as much for other groups.
Furthermore, the state ought to aid the farmers.
Such aid was essential to their continued existence
and would be a small compensation for the cheap food
they had provided the German people.[23]

In an analysis of these demands, two points
stand out. The first is the farmers' total conviction of the justice of their cause. They never
doubted that the state owed them something. The
state had previously come to their aid with the
tariff of 1879, thus freeing them from the unpleasant task of modernizing to meet foreign competition;
it had finally eliminated the wartime controls on
agricultural production; and once again, they
thought, "Father State" (*Vater Staat*) was morally
obligated to assist them. The outgoing *Regierungspräsident*, Adolf Johannsen, touched on this matter
in his report on the demonstrations of the twenty-
eighth of January. On the whole, he wrote, the farm
population had responded moderately to their situation; originally the expectation of state aid had
pacified them, but the delays in passing the emergency aid measure had evoked mistrust and disappoint-
ment with both the government and the farm interest
organizations. In Süderdithmarschen the National
Socialists had already exploited these feelings, and
the same could happen throughout the province unless
some aid were provided—an unfortunately accurate
prophecy. Johannsen, too, accepted the justice of
the farmers' claims and urged action on them.[24]

The second point to be noticed is the contrast
between Dithmarschen and the rest of Schleswig-
Holstein. In Dithmarschen speakers did not limit
themselves to economic demands, but proceeded to
clear attacks on the state; elsewhere nasty references to the Weimar regime did not lack, but the
tone was, on the whole, more moderate, and the
expectation of state aid still quite strong.

Numerous letters to the editors of farm journals
expressed the reluctance of many farmers to oppose
the state, but no one put the point more clearly
than one of Hans Fallada's "fictional" rebels in
Bauern, Bomben und Bonzen:

> You just don't know how hard it is to get these
> farmers in motion. When their farms are
> wrested out of their hands bit by bit, they
> gnash their teeth, but they knuckle under.
> "Those are the authorities (*die Obrigkeit*)"—
> that runs in their blood.[25]

Such sentiments, however, did not characterize the
proud, crusty, and volatile Dithmarschen farmers;
they were already in motion.

The Dithmarschen farmers, the most "radical" in
their analysis of the crisis, probably had the least
valid claim to state aid. Bad weather had ruined
crops and flooded marshes, but the poor management
of many Dithmarschen farmers had compounded the
effects of these natural catastrophes. The marsh
farmers had failed to keep abreast of their foreign
competition in the production of their goods, but
even more in the marketing of them. The Danes
undersold them on the Hamburg market with cows,
eggs, and butter of more consistent quality, but the
highly individualistic Dithmarscher refused to organize the sales cooperatives necessary to meet their
competition.[26] Easy profits during the years of
inflation had made them overconfident and content
with existing methods. Sure of future profits, they
used borrowed funds to purchase expensive luxury
items. One reporter commented that

> Almost everywhere one hears that most of the
> money obtained at that time through the mort-
> gage banks and other sources was invested inap-
> propriately or even frivolously, without the
> recipient's giving due attention to preserving
> his capital.[27]

Jokes about the foolish and inappropriate use of
loan funds abounded—perhaps the best evidence possible on the extent of this phenomenon.[28] In a
final fit of economic imprudence a number of
wealthy Dithmarschers had landed themselves in
difficulty through speculation on the exchanges.
These farmers, who themselves bore much of the

responsibility for their own misfortunes, played a
leading role in farm agitation.[29] As another of
Fallada's characters observes, "Look, Thiel, these
have always been rich farmers, living off the fat of
the land, and now they simply can't stomach it, when
they have to reign themselves in."[30]

Many of these wealthy farmers had supported
radical reaction well before their economic difficulties began. Thyge Thyssen, hardly a leftist
writer, discloses that Nazism had set roots in Dithmarschen long before the beginning of the depression:

> When Hitler in the first year after his release
> from the Landsberg prison (1923) announced a
> personal lecture in Hamburg, dozens of Dith-
> marschen farmers went to hear him—at first
> probably mostly out of curiosity. A partici-
> pant told the author that lists had been laid
> out on the tables in the hall. The speaker had
> pleased his audience and they had all signed
> up.[31] [Hitler did not leave Landsberg until
> 1924; however, the event Thyssen describes
> occurred—at the latest—in 1925, or well
> before the onset of the depression.]

A variety of reactionary militaristic groups had
prepared the ground for the Nazis. In 1920 the
Arbeitsgemeinschaft Dithmarschen, a quasi-military
organization formed to protect farmers against
thieves and Communist uprisings, attracted ten thousand members and ample funds from Norder- and Süderdithmarschen. The group had loose ties with the
notorious *Organisation Escherich*, and its leaders
did not hide their disgust with the new republic.
When the organization was dissolved, a number of
successor organizations formed. The personnel of
the banned *Arbeitsgemeinschaft* reassembled in veterans' clubs and nationalist societies. In February
1926, the most important of these successor organizations, *Wiking*, *Werwolf*, and the *Stahlhelm Westküste*—all nationalistic, militaristic, and anti-
Semitic in their orientation—merged in the *Wehr-
schaft Schleswig-Holstein*. From this organization
in turn came the leadership of the *Landvolkbewegung*.[32]

Radical reaction, then, was not a new phenomenon occasioned by the agricultural depression, but
an established political movement in Dithmarschen,
particularly among the larger farmers, as the fol-

lowing report of a farmers' meeting in Lunden by an
agent of the Flensburg criminal police shows:

> Those attending were composed on the one hand
> of large farmers who, as one could tell from
> the insignia they wore, belonged to associa-
> tions of the radical right. In their speeches
> and interjections they conducted themselves as
> enemies of the present regime. On the other
> hand there were the small farmers who in the
> course of the meeting showed themselves to be
> more reasonable, more insightful, and less
> opposed to the current government and the
> bureaucracy.[33]

This evidence runs counter to Heberle's views on the
political tradition of the larger Dithmarschen
farmers as a retarding factor in the growth of the
Nazi movement. The typical Nazi may not have been
a large farmer, but large farmers who were enemies
of the Republic long before the depression helped
introduce him to the party and its rhetoric.

Radical reaction had found a home in Dithmarschen, but it penetrated other areas of the province as well, although not to the same extent. In
the Geest area around Rendsburg, the *Tannenbergbund*
and *Werwolf* exploited an older anti-Semitism. In
Steinburg radical thrusts went out from the Ehrhardt
brigade, a malicious *Freikorps* band, which had been
settled in Lockstedter Lager and which became one of
the strong early nuclei of Nazism. In the northern
reaches of the province the *Schleswig-Holstein Bund*
stirred up irredentist sentiment. The wealthy landowners of East Holstein strongly supported the DNVP,
but not with the same ruthless abandon and lust for
violence that characterized the Dithmarschen extremists. Of all these areas only the region around
Lockstedter Lager in Steinburg really competed with
Dithmarschen as a center of radical reaction. Yet
within a few years rural areas other than Dithmarschen and Steinburg gave the Nazis equally large
or larger majorities. Why? Fundamental political
attitudes, the pressure of events, and the skillful
exploitation of these events by antirepublican
forces provide the answer.

The fundamental political attitudes of rural
Schleswig-Holsteiners did not dispose them to allegiance to a modern democratic regime like that of
the Weimar Republic. One can distinguish between

opposition to modern democracy *per se* and opposition
to the concrete form it assumed in the Germany of
the 1920s. Under the first category come local
particularism and suspicion of industrialization:
many rural Schleswig-Holsteiners looked askance at
the supposed benefits of absorption into Prussia and
rule by a centralized administration under Social
Democratic control rather than by staid local conservatives.

> At bottom, the criticism against Prussia was
> merely an expression of a general antipathy
> against the social system of industrial capi-
> talism, originating in a rural-conservative
> attitude, a criticism of society (*Gesellschaft*)
> out of a spirit of community (*Gemeinschaft*).
> The Prussian era, which had brought the great
> economic uplift for Schleswig-Holstein, was
> identified with the age of commercialization
> and industrialization, with the breakdown of
> good taste and the suffocation of creative and
> administrative activity in the province.[34]

The rural people longed for the simplicity of local
government in a nonindustrial setting, a privilege
areas of the province had enjoyed into the mid-nine-
teenth century. These men gave their allegiance to
an older world; they were reactionaries in the most
literal sense.
   Through industrialization and especially through
incorporation into Prussia the old rural elite had
lost its control over social change. It retained
local powers (even some of these were taken away),
but at the provincial and national level the Weimar
Republic gave it only the power to be outvoted in
the Prussian Landtag or the Reichstag. For the old
landholding elite the coming of democracy meant the
loss of political power, a state of affairs barely
tolerable in times of prosperity and an outrage in a
period of structural and cyclical economic crises.[35]
Democracy meant the ascendance of the new social
forces, industrial capital and labor, which brought
with them a threat to both the economic and the
political security of the rural propertied classes.
"Our farmers were never enthusiastic about the
Weimar Republic....They never felt at home in it."[36]
   The alienation of the rural upper and middle
classes from the Republic constituted a standing
danger in times of stress, as their behavior during

the Kapp putsch demonstrated. While the workers in
Kiel and on the East Holstein estates defended the
Republic by engaging in a general strike and even
small military clashes with the putschists, the
remainder of the rural population showed its disin-
clination to support Weimar democracy. The leaders
of the farm organizations (among them the *Landwirtschaftskammer*, the *Bund der Landwirte*, the *Bauernverein*, and the *Genossenschaftsverband*) expressed
their confidence in the new Kapp regime and threatened to cease supplying the cities with foodstuffs
should the general strike continue. *Freikorps* bands
skirmished with defenders of the Republic.[37] This
episode demonstrates how early the currents of rural
reaction merged with those of militarist nationalism
and hatred of socialism to pose an extremely grave
threat to the Republic.

The Republic's enemies nourished and propagated
these hostile attitudes. Thomas Mann, a native of
Lübeck, once remarked that "Conservative and national
are one and the same thing,"[38] and the two certainly
went together in Schleswig-Holstein. Conservatives
used the Versailles treaty and the loss of North
Schleswig as clubs to beat the Social Democrats.
The conservative forces built on the patriotic
propaganda of the war years, an indoctrination which
had left a deep mark on many young rural soldiers.
Organizations with strong nationalist tendencies
shot out of the ground—the *Landespartei*, the *Jung-
bauernbewegung*, the various *Bünde*, and the *Schleswig-Holstein Bund*, for example.[39] Eminently
"respectable" organizations cultivated the same
themes. The *Landbund* and the DNVP, the representatives of the large landed interests, kept up a constant flood of nationalist propaganda. The *Landwirtschaftskammer* repeatedly discussed the border
question.[40] Public and private organizations pursued the cultural struggle in North and South
Schleswig. Employers in the city of Schleswig fired
Danish sympathizers. And the barrage of nationalist
propaganda was effective; one SPD leader recalled
that when in rural electoral meetings he tried to
explain that North Schleswig was Danish, a great
roar, "*Nordschleswig ist deutsch*" ("North Schleswig
is German"), echoed through the hall.[41]

The Social Democrats' efforts at reconciliation
with Denmark were just one more reason for the
propertied classes to hate them. Class conflict,
papered over during the war, reopened once again at

its close as the SPD government continued to require
farmers to supply quotas of food for delivery to the
cities. The revolution in Kiel, and the Kapp putsch
divided the SPD and the rural property-holders into
two opposing camps; to the latter group the SPD
became identified with revolution and excesses
against property and the church. The lines of
political conflict were drawn; the abhorrence the
rural possessors felt for the socialist parties
became the decisive fact of rural political life.
Cooperation with the SPD branded a party as suspect
and brought it electoral disaster.[42]

Antisocialist sentiment had a decisive political consequence: when crisis came and the propertied classes sought new solutions, they would turn
to Fascism rather than to a leftist solution. Not
just one crisis, but a whole series came, and farmers, rural craftsmen, and merchants held the "Sozis"
and their Weimar "system" responsible. They thought
they had sufficient evidence for two conclusions:
the SPD-state had caused their troubles, and it had
caused them deliberately. They pointed to a whole
series of disastrous events: the "excesses" of
workers during the revolution, the prolongation of
oppressive wartime economy measures, the loss of
North Schleswig, the Versailles treaty, the SPD's
handling of the church education question in Schleswig-Holstein, the great inflation, and finally the
agricultural and industrial depression. For all
these catastrophes the Social Democrats and increasingly their bourgeois coalition partners and the
whole Weimar "system" were deemed responsible.

Up until the inflation there was perhaps some
prospect of eventually pacifying the rural landholders, but the inflation set off a train of social
processes which resulted in open rebellion and the
nearly total disaffection of the rural middle and
upper classes. Before 1924 farmers had benefited
from the inflation, but through a combination of
mismanagement and intrinsic difficulties they failed
to replace livestock, equipment, and other capital
used up in the war years; crop yields still lagged
behind those of prewar years.[43] The inflation had
wiped out previous indebtedness, but its stabiliza-
tion brought new and more serious difficulties. In
the fall of 1923 farmers sold much of their harvests
for old paper marks, but they had to pay taxes and
buy fertilizer and seed with the new *Rentenmark*. To
make these payments they had to borrow heavily and

at exorbitant rates; rates over 10 percent were not
uncommon. The comparisons are difficult and shaky,
but the actual level of debt does not seem to have
been appreciably higher than pre-1914 levels; however, the interest burden was heavier and, combined
with higher tax burdens on farm property, began to
squeeze the farmer. The margin of safety in case of
a bad harvest, a flood, or a fall in prices disappeared. The call for aid went out from the agricultural interest organizations.[44]

The farmers' new difficulties provided further
ammunition for opponents of the Republic. Already
the leaders of farm interest organizations had been
assailing the Republic and urging their followers
into the ranks of the oppositionists of the radical
right.[45] Now they seized upon the lack of state aid
as conclusive evidence of the perfidy of the "system." Using the same arguments, right extremist
groups flourished:

> The relatively quiet years from 1925 to 1927
> were precisely the period in which these new
> mass organizations consolidated their movements
> on a broader basis and secured a decisive
> influence on the formation of opinion among
> very large sections of the population.[46]

The agricultural interest organizations had conjured
up a threat to themselves; the new groups began to
question the utility of interest organizations which
could not extract aid from the state. These new
movements argued that new forms of political action
were required—at the least a unification of the
agricultural interest groups, hitherto split between
the *Landbund*, the *Bauernverein*, and an organization
of very small farmers.

The demonstrations of January 28, 1928, had
produced a joint committee of these farm organizations which was headed by Otto Johannsen. The committee was dispatched to Berlin to petition and
negotiate for aid.

> At the beginning of 1928 people still expected
> help from the national government and thought
> that the agricultural crisis could be overcome
> if the representatives friendly to agriculture
> and the lobbyists under the leadership of Otto
> Johannsen would respectfully and energetically
> point out the acute distress in Schleswig
> Holstein.[47]

The delegation met with Reich agricultural minister
Schiele and others, and secured a promise of assistance; but Schiele's actions did not meet the farmers' expectations.[48] The government's emergency
program came less rapidly and provided less gener-
ously than the farmers had hoped. The government
appropriated 30 million marks to shore up the price
of hogs, but otherwise failed to offer much satisfaction. It provided 3.4 million marks in loans to
Schleswig-Holstein farms (well under the 5 million
marks it spent on irredentist schemes in North
Schleswig in 1926), and at an interest rate of 9
percent. Even a Danish historian concedes that the
emergency measures did not go very far.[49]

If Johannsen's effort had had little success,
the traditional interest organizations did no better.
Their lobbying produced no new assistance. Their
electoral advice fared even worse. In 1928 the
Committee of Six, a directorate composed of leaders
from the most important agricultural interest groups,
recommended that farmers vote for the three bourgeois parties rather than the new farmers' parties
or the NSDAP. When the DDP, DVP, and DNVP lost
forty-three seats and the Nazis and the farmers'
parties gained substantially, the interest group
representatives lost their remaining credit with the
farm population.[50] Now the rural people beyond
Dithmarschen began to ask embarrassing and dangerous
questions:

> "What good is a *Bauernverein*, a *Landbund*, a
> Chamber of Agriculture, when in such obviously
> catastrophic circumstances even their long-
> established leaders can't push through an
> effective program in Berlin?" asked farmers on
> all sides.[51]

Nor was it just the interest organizations that were
held responsible.

If farm representatives failed to obtain aid,
then the state and its representatives must not want
to aid them—so reasoned many farmers. They noted
that the SPD newspapers had refused to admit the
possibility of an agrarian crisis and that the new
Kiel program had not erased the conviction of the
SPD membership that all farmers were conniving
Junkers at heart—was that not further evidence that
no help could be expected from such a state?
Respectable DNVP representatives and a host of more
radical agitators constantly reiterated the message

that the "Reds" were the farmers' implacable enemies.
They identified the state and the socialist parties
with each other and made them responsible for the
farmers' economic troubles.

Regierungspräsident Johannsen summarized the
evolution of farmers' attitudes in a report dated
March 9, 1928. This important document provides a
useful sketch of the state of rural opinion:

> Originally the wait for the passage of the
> emergency program and complementary measures by
> the national and provincial governments had
> occasioned a certain feeling of hope and confi-
> dence that agriculture would in fact be helped
> as much as possible, a feeling which still
> persists in many places and which is cultivated
> by the agricultural interest organizations.
> But in other areas, and especially in the most
> rural areas, instead of this hope a feeling of
> widespread disappointment and irritation has
> appeared because there people assume that the
> promises made will not be kept and that all the
> parleying of the farm organizations is use-
> less....Also not to be denied is the fact that
> the central government's lengthy delay in
> taking measures to alleviate the distress of
> the agricultural population has contributed and
> continues to contribute to an inclination
> toward general destructive criticism of all
> phases of our public life among the rural
> population, even among the prudent and sensible
> farmers....This mood makes them susceptible to
> radical influences and thus it has been
> observed that in Süderdithmarschen, for exam-
> ple, National Socialist agitation is
> spreading.[52]

The tardiness and inadequacy of state aid opened a
new phase in the evolution of rural opinion. From
this point on the slogan "Against the parties and
without the farm organizations" gained in popu-
larity.[53]

The Nazis did not gather in the discontented
without opposition. In the Rendsburg area the
Tannenbergbund offered stiff competition. But their
greatest rival was that remarkable phenomenon, the
Landvolkbewegung. The *Landvolk* movement originated
in the summer of 1928 as farmers began to refuse to
pay taxes and attempted to prevent foreclosures. On

the nineteenth of November a group of farmers
succeeded in preventing the seizure of cattle from
two farmers at Beidenfleth; this incident supplied
the decisive impulse for the movement. A week later
farmers demonstrated in Itzehoe and bombs exploded
at the homes of government officials in Telling-
stedt, Flehderwürth, and Beidenfleth. Repudiation
of parliamentary procedures in favor of direct
action, rural solidarity against foreclosures and
attachment, and bombings intended to intimidate
rather than to kill—these were the tactics of the
Landvolk movement. The precise objectives of the
movement were less than clear. The dominant thrust
was for self-administration; if only farmers and
rural people could govern themselves, the *Landvolk*
leaders reasoned, they could avoid the mistakes of
socialists and bureaucrats.
     The tactics of the *Landvolk* movement challenged
the state directly and in late 1928 and early 1929 a
series of trials against *Landvolk* adherents for
refusal to pay taxes and resistance to state authorities began. These trials provided a perfect forum
for antirepublican propaganda. In the courtroom the
defense lawyer, Luetgebrune, put the state itself on
trial. Farmers throughout the province sensed the
very appearance of their fellows in the courts as
rank injustice. One farmer expressed the prevalent
opinion in a letter to the *Landbote*: "When these
farmers [the defendants] are driven to desperation
and act accordingly, then it is an offense against
God and against the law of man—if such a thing
still exists—to send them to prison."[54]
     The forcible foreclosures and seizures and the
trials of those who resisted them completed the
process of convincing the farmers that the state was
their enemy. The speech of Vadder Benthin, an old
farmer in Fallada's fictional treatment of the *Landvolk* movement, expresses the farmers' feelings of
frustration and betrayal: "The whole state has done
us in. Before we had enough to live on; today....I'd
just like to see how you'd like it, to have a man in
uniform come and drag your cattle out of their
stalls."[55] *Landvolk* agitators roamed throughout the
province and into East Prussia, Pomerania, Silesia,
Hannover, Oldenburg, Saxony, and Thuringia publi-
cizing the fate of the movement's martyrs and urging
farmers to resist by refusing to pay taxes.[56]
     Geographically the movement's support in
Schleswig-Holstein lay in southern Holstein, Süder-

dithmarschen, around Itzehoe, and especially on the
border between the Geest and the marshes. In
Schleswig and the eastern hill region the movement
gained few adherents; but even where it did not
enlist members, it succeeded in altering opinions.
In an enlightening report the *Landrat* of Kreis Plön
recalled a conversation with two farmers in the tiny
village of Grossbarkau on April 26, 1929. The two
threatened nonpayment of taxes.

> They said that the farmers in Beidenfleth had
> gotten things started and that they were going
> to join in. I suggested that the Beidenfleth
> matter concerned local taxes. Thereupon Kühl
> and Johannes Riecken said, "That was only a
> means to an end; they turned against the system
> and we will too." Johs. Riecken added: "As
> long as there are oak clubs around, I'm not
> going to be driven off my farm." Kühl expressed
> himself along similar lines. Johs. Riecken
> said, "Before I was very conservative, but now
> I'm thoroughly radical."[57]

The lack of state aid, the trials, and the propaganda of the *Landvolk* and the Nazis had succeeded
in driving out the remaining traces of reverence and
respect for "*Obrigkeit.*"
    Politically the *Landvolk* movement maintained
the closest ties with the nationalist opposition and
antirepublican extremists. Its leaders, Hamkens,
Heim, Nickels, and Volck, were hardly the disinter-
ested men forced into politics by public spirited-
ness and outrage against evil that the *Landvolk*'s
propaganda pictured them to be; all had been prominent members of the virulently antirepublican and
militaristic *Stahlhelm-Westküste*. They had links to
and strong support from both the local DNVP and the
Landbund. But the movement eschewed any effort at
careful organization. Its leaders equated organization with bureaucratic lethargy and inertia—and
organization eased the state's task of discovering
its enemies. The *Landvolk* confined themselves to a
few loose committees and a newspaper, *Das Landvolk*.
From its offices in Itzehoe *Das Landvolk* poured
forth a vitriolic flood of anti-Semitic and antirepublican propaganda essentially indistinguishable
from that of the Nazis.
    The *Landvolk* movement helped politicize the
economic crisis still further and it prepared the

way for the Nazis, but it never threatened to take
power itself; indeed its lack of organization
rendered such an attempt impossible. The movement
continued to espouse radical goals, but never developed the machinery necessary to accomplish its
aims. For all its vivid rhetoric the movement could
not show the farmers any concrete achievement of its
own; when modest state aid came, it took the steam
out of the movement. The *Landvolk* collected substantial dues, but spent them primarily on lavish
legal fees. As more and more *Landvolk* leaders
landed in jail, the farmers became disenchanted.

> Rural people said that they didn't know why
> they should pay such high dues or what the
> *Landvolk* movement did with all the money.
> They thought that in Itzehoe and elsewhere too
> many people wanted to live off the "dumb
> farmers'" money.[58]

The failure of demonstrations, boycotts of forced
auctions, and tax strikes to generate a revolutionary
movement drove one wing of the *Landvolk* group under
Heim and Volck to more desperate tactics. In the
summer of 1929 a series of bombings shattered public
buildings in Itzehoe, Niebüll, Schleswig, and elsewhere in North Germany. In early September police
seized one of the conspirators as he was transport-
ing a bomb. Within forty-eight hours his coconspir-
ators had been rounded up and arrested. The *Landvolk* movement was effectively finished; it staggered
on for another two or three years, but with little
success. Its lack of organization and its chaotic
tactics condemned it to failure.

Hans Beyer has recently tried to rehabilitate
the *Landvolk* movement. In a series of articles and
pamphlets he has argued that one has to distinguish
the *völkisch* movement from the Nazis. Beyer, who
during the Weimar period had worked on *Landvolk*
publications and edited another rightist sheet,
argues that the *Landvolk's* struggle against the
NSDAP demonstrates its innocence. Beyer prefers to
emphasize the particularist, corporatist themes in
the movement and its opposition to all political
parties. Beyer's arguments are often oblique and
his evidence is minimal; his case for a sharp distinction between *Landvolk* and Nazis is simply not
convincing. The archives abound with reports of
discouraged *Landvolk* men going over to the Nazis.

Here are just a few samples of such reports:

Berlin criminal police [*Norderdithmarschen, March 1929*]:
> ....Today the *Landvolk* movement and the *Wach-vereinigung* (a branch of the *Landvolk*) have only a secondary importance; the former members of these two organizations have turned their backs on them and fled in droves to the NSDAP. Thus, for example, the forty-man *Wachvereinigung* contingent in Büsum joined the NSDAP en masse.[59]

Berlin police [*Süderdithmarschen, April 1929*]:
> As already noted above, in many cases the adherents of the "*Landvolk* movement" have become members of the "NSDAP." People saw that the *Landvolk* movement was unable to bring about a change in the economic situation and now hope that the National Socialists will fulfill their wishes. People generally hold the view that the current political system alone is responsible for the bad economic situation and hope for the coming of a revolution through the National Socialists.[60]

Berlin police [*Schleswig, April 1929*]:
> *Landvolk* movement: Its supporters have changed over to the NSDAP.[61]

Berlin police [*Husum, April 1929*]:
> The members of the local [*Wachvereinigung*] organizations have for the most part transferred over to the local organizations of the NSDAP.[62]

One could multiply these bits of evidence, but that is unnecessary. Beyer himself contradicts his own position by arguing Ernst von Salomon's case in *Fragebogen*. There von Salomon argues that the Berlin special police drove farmers out of the *Landvolk* into the clutches of the Nazis. But to blame the Berlin police for the success of Nazism is patently absurd. What happened was that the *völkisch* conservatives conjured up a monster they could not handle. Ultimately the *Landvolk* leaders may have opposed the Nazis, but they made an invaluable contribution to their success.

The Nazis did not need a great deal of help. Only one bourgeois newspaper in the entire province

opposed them. At their public meetings they encoun-
tered little opposition except from a few Communists, who probably made more Nazis than they
dissuaded. The whole movement was astoundingly well
organized; in October 1929, the party held 115 meetings, an unprecedented feat of political organizing,
particularly when one adds the preparations for SA
marches and the like. But in 1930 and 1931 the
party would hold well over 200 meetings in some
months; it would organize local units and SA troops
in the remotest villages. And always the party
presented the image of an irresistible force, a
political army whose march could not be stopped.

The NSDAP in Schleswig-Holstein originated in
the cities. From these urban centers the movement
began in late 1926 and in 1927 to propagandize and
organize on the Dithmarscher Geest, around Lockstedter Lager, and among the hog farmers of Steinburg and Pinneberg. Here the party scored its first
electoral successes in 1928. In the next years the
party systematically worked its way through Dithmarschen, southern Holstein, and the Geest area,
slowly expanding its activities northward and east-
ward. The 3,000 members of 1928 grew to 42,000 by
the end of 1931, the highest percentage of NSDAP
members to population in the country.[63]

The Nazis' most conspicuous successes came in
the regions with the greatest communal solidarity
and the least class antagonism, the Geest and
Angeln. There the party could more easily switch
the allegiance of an entire village and enforce its
supremacy against all but the most prestigious
dissenters; the greater similarity of interests and
the tighter forms of social control permitted a
degree of success unattainable in less homogeneous
villages. The sharper class distinctions of Dithmarschen and East Holstein posed a barrier to Nazi
gains; the party might recruit every small property
holder in a village, but fail to enlist much support
from the working class or from estate owners.

Where the Nazis won early backers among the
rural elite, they rapidly gained new members; the
party recognized this fact and prominently featured
Lutheran clergymen and local notables among its
speakers and organizers. An early turn to Nazism,
as on the west coast, allowed the old elite to
retain its dominant local position. In sections of
Dithmarschen the Nazis' control of local government
created a true crisis of state authority; the

republican authorities feared to remove less offensive Nazi officials from office for fear that worse
ones might replace them. Where on the other hand
the local elite resisted Nazi appeals, they managed
to retard Nazi incursions, but eventually they were
swept out of office by a reaction from below and
consigned to ignominy.

     In an effort to trace more carefully and to
quantify the effects of rural social organization
upon political developments, I tried to discover how
many local Nazi leaders were prominent landholders,
employing the names and data presented in the
government's reports on Nazi personnel and the
information on rural property owners contained in
Niekammer's Guide to Rural Landholders.[64] The
results of this investigation were inconclusive, but
they do show a strong component of large landowners
among the Nazi organizers. Of 294 Nazi leaders in
rural communities in 1929-30, 58—or about a sixth—
were large landowners in their communities. A somewhat greater number held nonagricultural, middle-
class jobs. For two reasons these figures probably
underestimate considerably the importance of the
rural elite: First, the government's information
does not always appear to have been correct; thus
some large landowners may not be properly identified
and thus cannot be found in *Niekammer's*. Second,
and more important, the local elite may have dele-
gated organizing responsibilities to others they
deemed more suited for the task.

     As the NSDAP gained in numbers and power it
both infiltrated interest group organizations and
converted the members of these organizations. On
August 20, 1931, the party encouraged its members to
join the *Land-und-Bauernbund*, the largest and most
important farm organization to emerge from the
amalgamation efforts of January 1928.[65] The success
of this tactic is indicated by the *Bund's* support of
Hitler in the presidential election of 1932, "without yielding nonpartisanship in principle," as the
Bund put it.[66] So thoroughly Nazified did the organization become that it was absorbed into the Nazi
administrative apparatus rather than dissolved like
the oppositionist rump of the old *Bauernverein*. One
would be hard pressed to attribute the Nazis'
triumph to their manipulative abilities; the old
farm leaders were hurrying to get on the bandwagon.

     Among the rural craftsmen the pressure for
Nazification of the interest groups also came from
below.

The leaders and membership of the provincial
and county [*Kreis*] craft organizations first
shrank back from political radicalism and held
themselves aloof from the NSDAP. Only in the
middle of 1931 did a political regrouping come
about. The impetus came from below, from the
local and county organizations, which were now
directed exclusively by the NSDAP.[67]

The Nazis' success among the middle classes was,
then, remarkably complete.

Where the party did not obtain complete success
by persuasion, it employed terror. The Nazis said
they fought "with the fist and with the power of the
word," and by 1932 the accent often seemed to be on
the former. They described their movement as an
avalanche that smashed everything that stood in its
way, and the instances of terror from 1928 to 1934
lend melancholy testimony to the truth of their
assertion.[68] The party early threatened to boycott
nonmembers in areas where it was strong; National
Socialists in Dithmarschen refused to hire servants
and farm workers who were not party members. In one
case a Meldorf beer distributor and party leader
used a boycott to put a competitor out of business.
The SA broke up opponents' meetings; they prevented
the showing of *All Quiet on the Western Front*. When
all else failed, the Nazis murdered their enemies
in the most brutal fashion.

Excessive violence had helped discredit the
Landvolk movement, but it brought the Nazis new
recruits. When the Nazis beat Communists to death
in the marsh hamlet of Wöhrden, their membership
totals leaped. The rural people of Schleswig-
Holstein showed a considerable tolerance for the
political violence of the Nazis; to say that they
had no indication of what the Nazis would do when
once in power assumes a remarkable blindness to the
systematic terror the Nazis exercised before they
came to power. The Nazis were clever enough to
concentrate on Communists, who enjoyed about as much
sympathy in rural Schleswig-Holstein as Abbie
Hoffman would at a DAR convention. They professed
their adherence to parliamentary methods and blamed
all scuffles on their opponents. The bourgeois
press in the province all but unanimously supported
the Nazi interpretation, a fact which mitigates but
does not excuse popular acceptance of National
Socialist terror. The rural landowners accepted the
Nazi argument that their only choice was Nazism or

Communism, and they picked Nazism, many with enthusiasm, some out of resignation.

The Nazi triumph, then, was not the result of
economic depression, but of economic depression
interpreted in the categories of nationalist reaction. The NSDAP's success was the more thorough the
more a village approximated a *Gemeinschaft* of homogeneous petty bourgeois. The landowners and craftsmen of rural Schleswig-Holstein chose to explain
their economic difficulties as the result of the
machinations of international bankers, Jews, and
Socialists rather than as the outcome of severe
structural and cyclical crises and poor harvests
caused by bad weather. The reactionary nationalists
who had never reconciled themselves to a defeated
and democratic republic succeeded in politicizing
economic difficulties. They played upon the deep-
rooted conservative, nationalist, and anti-Marxist
prejudices of the rural population and drowned out
those few scattered voices who called for a
rational adjustment in economic policies and structures. The bourgeois parties either joined them or
remained silent. The government and the socialist
parties eased the task of the radical agitators by
refusing to take the farmers' difficulties seri-
ously. Under these circumstances the brilliant
propagandists and organizers of the Nazi party—for
one has to recognize their genius while allowing
for its evil inspiration—succeeded in five years in
persuading or terrorizing 63.8 percent of the rural
population into voting for them.
It should be noted, finally, that these events
contradict the mass society explanation of Nazi
success just as thoroughly as they refute the simple
economic explanation. To argue, as William Kornhauser does, that within all social classes "those
[people] with the fewest social ties are the most
receptive to mass appeals"[69] is simply wrong; the
Nazis triumphed most thoroughly precisely where
social ties were strongest—in the organic communities of the Schleswig Geest. The rural people of
Schleswig-Holstein were not atomistic individuals;
they had organized themselves into well-articulated
interest groups. These attachments to secondary
associations did not prevent Nazi incursions, however—indeed the farm interest groups' failure to
satisfy farmers' economic demands contributed
greatly to the Nazis' advance. When rural Schleswig-

Holsteiners went over to the NSDAP, they did so not
as isolated individuals, but as members of farm
organizations, patriotic societies, and organic
communities. It is true that the bourgeois parties'
failure to develop local organizations in rural
areas facilitated Nazi recruitment, but in general
it was not the absence of secondary associations,
but the character of those present, that aided the
Nazi cause. "A plurality of independent groups
supports liberty at the same time that it supports
authority"[70] only where these independent groups are
firmly attached to the prevailing political regime;
but in rural Schleswig-Holstein the farm interest
organizations, the DNVP, the veterans' groups, the
Schleswig-Holstein Bund, the *völkisch* societies, and
numerous other organizations fostered the growth of
oppositional sentiments and prepared the rural population to interpret the depression in categories
favorable to the Nazi cause.

3: Changes in the Political Infrastructure, 1933-1970

Any serious effort to compare the position of a contemporary neo-Nazi party with the position of the Nazi party in the Weimar Republic must include a survey of the remarkable changes in the rural political environment. A static comparative analysis which neglected the alterations in demographic, economic, political, and psychological structures between 1933 and the present would be ahistorical and misleading. Similarly any analysis which ignored the new configuration of economic and political forces would fail to expose the conditions under which a present-day neo-Nazi party must operate. Therefore, in order to illuminate the origins and character of the politics of the present, it becomes necessary to sketch briefly the most important historical changes of the intervening period.

After a brief consideration of an embarrassing gap in the account, caused by the lack of solid evidence about shifts in public opinion under the Nazi regime, the analysis of this chapter turns first to the enormous alteration in Schleswig-Holstein's demographic structure resulting from the huge influx of refugees at the war's end. There follows a short summary of the crucial changes in the underlying economic and social structure, the decline in the importance of agriculture and the concomitant homogenization of peculiarities of regional societies. Finally the remodeling of the electoral system, the emergence of a new set of political parties, and the new winds in the "polit-

ical atmosphere" indicated by the results of postwar
elections come under scrutiny.

It is impossible to trace adequately developments in public opinion under the Nazi regime
because there are no good sources for the period
from 1933 to 1945. Before 1933 Nazi terror and
intimidation had prevented open expression of political opinion in many parts of the countryside, and
following 1933 these pressures intensified. The
opportunity and the means for expressing dissenting
opinions disappeared. The leaders of other parties
emigrated or disappeared into concentration camps.
The remaining centers of resistance tottered and
fell. "Before the onset of the war most of the
illegal groups had already been brought to a stand-
still through the drafting of their members into
labor service, military service, relief works, and
the like."[1]

Withholding one's ballot in the Nazi elections
was futile; the local Nazi election official simply
reported a 100 percent turnout for the NSDAP regard-
less.[2] Even the reports of the Nazi *Gauleiter* give
only a rough measure of the general rise and fall of
support for the regime; consequently estimates of
the state of public opinion from 1933 to 1945 must
remain highly speculative. Perhaps the safest
generalization is that until the hard days of
impending defeat in the war no real mass disenchantment with Nazism began; but as the catastrophe of
total defeat became inescapable, the population cast
the blame upon Hitler and his party. They had abdi-
cated all responsibility to the *Führer* a decade
before, and now they held him totally responsible.[3]
The ensuing Allied revelations of Nazi atrocities
against the Jews genuinely shocked many and occasioned some real remorse. There was, then, disillu-
sionment with Nazism shortly after the war's end,
but again in this period historical sources are
unavailable—no one in rural Schleswig-Holstein
could afford to take time off from the business of
staying alive to conduct an opinion poll.

The postwar influx of refugees is the first
outstanding feature distinguishing the periods
before 1933 and after 1945. In the hundred years
before 1945 the population of Schleswig-Holstein had
increased by slightly over 800,000 to roughly
1,600,000; in the four years 1945-1948 the population rose by over a million. Even these figures do
not portray the rapidity with which refugees poured

into Schleswig-Holstein at the end of the war; in
the four-month period from February to June 1945 the
population soared from 1,645,700 to 2,435,000.[4]
(Table III-1 shows the pace of this movement.) By
1949 the flow had still not completely abated, but
from then on the movement of refugees out into other
areas of the Bundesrepublik began to exceed the
number of those newly locating in Schleswig-Holstein.

Table III-1

*The Arrival of Refugees and Evacuees
in Schleswig-Holstein*

Year	Number	
1939-42	2,784	
1943	38,326	
1944	16,515	
1945	553,602	
1946	313,532	
1947	77,144	
1948	56,405	
plus	46,341	children born to refugees in Schleswig-Holstein
total	1,104,649	

Source: *Die Flüchtlinge in Schleswig-Holstein*
           (Sonderheft F of the *Statistischen
           Monatshefte Schleswig-Holstein*),
           p. 9.

The greatest portion of the refugees came from
the former provinces of Pomerania and East Prussia.
The 1949-50 census showed 338,007 from Pomerania and
329,606 from East Prussia, respectively 30.6 and
29.8 percent of all refugees in Schleswig-Holstein.
The remainder came from all corners of Eastern
Europe, from the former provinces of Brandenburg and
Silesia, from Danzig, Memel, and the Sudetenland,
from Poland, the Soviet Union, and the countries of
southeastern Europe.[5] Just over one quarter of the
refugee working population had previously been
engaged in agriculture, another fourth in industry,
a fifth in trade and communications, an eighth in
administration; nurses, doctors, intellectuals of

various stripes, and a smattering of other occupations completed the list. Contrary to a belief prevalent in the early postwar period, the age distribution of the incoming population was favorable. Whereas 15.3 percent of the native population were sixty or over, only 10.6 percent of the refugees were; similarly the refugee population showed a slightly greater concentration in the eighteen to thirty-five age bracket (23.0 to 20.1 percent).[6]

The first need of the refugees was housing. So pressing was the situation that the fleeing population had to be assigned living space with no attention to the suitability of their skills to the economic structure of the stipulated area. The resulting "misallocation" led to a high degree of internal migration within Schleswig-Holstein as people sought out areas where their particular skills might be employed; thus in addition to the wave of immigrant refugees, there came a second wave of movement within (and out of) Schleswig-Holstein— not to mention the higher-than-average rate of relocation by the native population.[7] At no time did the influx of refugees spread out evenly over the *Land*. At first they concentrated near their points of arrival and where shelter was available; later they moved to the areas with the healthiest economies—those which could provide jobs.

From 1946 the various *Land* regimes in Schleswig-Holstein pursued two basic policies in order to cope with the refugee question. First, they sought to convince the British occupation authorities, and later the Bonn government, that Schleswig-Holstein was bearing an undue portion of the refugee burden, and that consequently refugees ought to be resettled in other *Ländern* and supplementary payments made to the Kiel regime. The economy of Schleswig-Holstein, they rightly argued, simply could not cope with problems of such scope. The agricultural sector could absorb few additional workers over the long term, and the dismantling of armaments plants and ship works, a large part of the industrial economy, eliminated about 90,000 jobs directly or indirectly.[8] Neither employment opportunities nor a tax base commensurate with the need existed. When suggestions that Schleswig-Holstein be merged with Hamburg and Niedersachsen came to naught, the Kiel government had no alternative but to lobby for a federal policy to equalize the burdens of assimilating the refugees.

At the same time, Schleswig-Holstein governments pursued a second line of policy: they tried
to expand the local economy and integrate the refugees into it. This effort involved getting rid of
some cumbersome ideological baggage. Schleswig-
Holstein had long had the reputation of being an
agricultural area. At the beginning of the 1950s
the president of the *Landesbauernkammer* was still
muttering nonsense about Schleswig-Holstein's
remaining an *"Agrarland,"* "so that in periods of
crisis we will still have a nutritional basis for
our people, one which will suffice to feed our population from its own resources in difficult conditions."[9] The glorification of agriculture was most
dangerous when it was combined with a positive
animosity to industry, as it had been in a 1941
speech by the *Landeshauptmann* Dr. Schow:

> Schleswig-Holstein has always had a predomi-
> nantly agricultural character. It should
> retain it. Factories and plants with hundreds
> or even thousands of employees have no claim
> on land in our district.[10]

Now, however, the CDU and the SPD both challenged
the old conception and not only placed land at
industry's disposal, but provided low-interest
loans, special freight tariffs, and tax advantages
as well. Nonetheless, the settling of new industry
in Schleswig-Holstein was a slow process, as the
employment figures show (see table III-2).
    The effort to create employment opportunities
in the agricultural sector is not a brilliant
chapter in the history of Schleswig-Holstein. The
government of Schleswig-Holstein did not need to
promote the use of refugees as farm laborers; the
local farmers were smart enough to recognize a
favorable opportunity when it appeared. Lenchen
Rehders' contemporary account of the situation in
the East Holstein farm village of Fiefbergen
described other areas as well, and especially those
areas where manorial agriculture prevailed.

> Certain economic advantages accrued to the
> farms through the refugees' invasion into the
> villages. Since the refugees filled in the
> farm labor shortage that had been caused by
> the war, the farmer was spared a shortage of
> laborers that would surely have developed in

Table III-2

Unemployment in Schleswig-Holstein 1949-1952

Date (Sept.)	Total Unemployed	As percentage of Labor Force	Total Unemployed Refugees	As percentage of all unemployed
1949	187,300	22.2	110,600	59
1950	178,100	21.5	101,100	57
1951	156,900	19.9	83,800	53
1952	118,900	15.4	60,700	51

Source: Handbuch für Schleswig-Holstein (Kiel, 1955), p. 410. Cited in Varain,
Parteien und Verbände, p. 13.

> the normal course of events. With respect to
> the acquisition of workers the farmer actually
> enjoyed an advantage in comparison with prewar
> conditions. Today he is in position of being
> able to choose his help from a large number of
> applicants and hence to make a qualitative
> selection, whereas before the war he was
> compelled to employ anyone who applied simply
> in order to have help.[11]

Farm laborers, however, had and still have extremely
low status and income in West Germany, and it was
natural that many formerly independent farmers
pressed for farmsteads of their own.

Conservative circles vocally supported these
demands, praising the stabilizing influence of the
independent farmer—a truly astounding argument
after the 1928-33 experience—and even arguing that
Germany would need a reserve of farmers when it
reacquired the lost lands in the east![12] The
government ought not to create these farmsteads at
the expense of large landowners, however; SPD
efforts to limit holdings to 100 hectares were
delayed and emasculated until in 1949 the large
landowners, in a shrewd tactical move, offered
30,000 hectares for refugee settlements—on terms
favorable to them. The land was then divided into
plots small enough to settle 10,000 refugees and
about a third as many natives—and too small to
prove economically tenable fifteen to twenty years
later.[13] In short, the regime's efforts to create
jobs for the refugees in industry and agriculture
were inadequate; the resettlement of refugees outside
Schleswig-Holstein, which took place in increasing
numbers after 1949, was indispensable. It was
unfortunate for Schleswig-Holstein that the most
energetic and capable young workers tended to
migrate, leaving older pensioners behind.

The enormous demographic changes occasioned by
the swarm of refugees did not—in the long run—
alter basic features of the political landscape.
The newcomers interrupted, but did not break, the
patterns of the old rural society. The growth of
industry proceeded from the old centers around
Hamburg, in Lübeck, and in the Kiel-Rendsburg-Neu-
münster area, and while the growing urban wealth
exerted a strong attraction in rural areas, luring
workers and consumers in greater numbers than ever
before, the basic political cleavages remained
intact.

This continuity and persistence of traditional
structures is the theme of Ulrich Matthée's historical study of local political elites.[14]   Although
limited to one "county" (*Kreis*), and slightly exag-
gerating the degree of permanence. Matthée's conclusion catches an essential element of rural politics
in Schleswig-Holstein:

> Not only the principles of communal elite
> formation, but the elites themselves have been
> little touched by the great historical convul-
> sions of this century which have brought such
> sharp changes at the national level. Practi-
> cally speaking, the elites have perpetuated
> their dominance with only minor interruptions
> over a period extending from at least a hundred
> years ago into the most recent past. Neither
> the population increase after 1945 nor the
> industrialization of the county that coincided
> with it could endanger the rule of the old
> elites; just as little could changes in the
> form of government, manipulation of the elec-
> toral law and municipal constitution, or the
> massive intervention of the occupying powers
> shake their position. Although modern tech-
> nology has revolutionized agricultural
> patterns, the traditional hierarchical social
> order of the farm villages has remained largely
> inviolate. Today, as previously, the families
> at the top of the social pyramid lay successful
> claims to the positions of political leader-
> ship.[15]

The old structures and organization of rural society
have indeed endured, but the impact of the rural
community on society as a whole has diminished as
the importance of agriculture has declined.
     This decline in the importance of agriculture
is the second great historical change from the era
of the Great Depression to the present. Nazism did
not arrest social change, as many of its lower
middle-class followers had hoped, and the 1950s and
1960s brought still more rapid structural changes.
Whereas in 1925 and 1933 30 percent of the work
force engaged in agriculture, in 1950 only 25
percent and in 1961 only 16 percent did. This movement out of agriculture coincided with an expansion
of the labor force in industry, transport, communications, and services. Not only did the agricultural work force decline relatively; it fell abso-

lutely. From 1933 to 1961 the number of those
working in agriculture fell from 231,000 to
157,900.[16] The reduction of the agricultural labor
force occurred primarily among dependent farm
workers; between 1939 and 1961 the number of farm
workers dropped from 73,700 to 43,200, but the
number of independent farm proprietors decreased by
only 1,400 from 49,200 to 47,800.[17] These asymmet-
rical reductions have resulted in a restructuring of
the farm population, as Table III-3 illustrates.
The farm worker is a disappearing figure in rural
society; he is departing agriculture for more remu-
nerative urban pursuits, leaving the countryside to
the family farmer.

      The trend toward the family farm is unmistak-
able; not only have the largest farms (over a
hundred hectares) greatly reduced their work forces,
the number of very small farms (under twenty hectares) has dropped sharply and the rate of their
decline is accelerating. From 1949 to 1969 no fewer
than 12,762 farms of this size were abandoned, or
about 670 a year.[18] From 1968 the number of farms
between twenty and thirty hectares also began to
decline, indicating that the disappearance of
marginal farms and the amalgamation of productive
units is continuing apace. These developments have
not been confined to a limited geographic area, but
have occurred in all three natural regions. As
early as 1961 an official statistician was drawing
the obvious conclusion: "The family farm has spread
with elemental force as the outstanding form of
agricultural operations in Schleswig-Holstein."[19]

      Along with the decline in the rural labor force
and the movement toward the family farm have come
enormous increases in agricultural productivity. No
other industry has been able to match agriculture in
this respect. From 1950 to 1961, for example, the
agricultural sector of Schleswig-Holstein's economy
expanded at an average yearly rate of 10 percent—
well above the industrial sector's 7 percent, and at
a time of substantial reduction in the labor
force.[20] Through the employment of machinery rather
than human labor, farmers in Schleswig-Holstein have
become far more efficient, and with their increased
efficiency and productivity have come sizable gains
in income, though farmers complain bitterly that
these gains do not adequately compensate them for
their productive improvements and—still worse—lag
behind the raises of urban workers. Nonetheless,

Table III-3

Changes in Farm Population 1949-1965

	1949		1956		1960		1965	
Owners	48,500	20%	43,772	24%	39,100	26%	36,099	29%
Family Help	95,625	38%	76,441	43%	71,345	48%	61,295	49%
Hired Help	103,386	42%	58,263	33%	39,118	26%	27,446	22%

Source: Statistisches Landesamt Schleswig-Holstein, *Statistische Monatshefte Schleswig-Holstein*, Jg. 18, Heft 3 (1966), p. 56.

the combined effect of these recent trends in agriculture has been to make Schleswig-Holstein's
farmers considerably less numerous and far more
prosperous than they were a half century ago.

Governmental policy has consciously advanced
these changes in the agricultural economy. The 1955
Agricultural Law committed the federal government to
ensuring that agriculture participated in the
general progress of the German economy; the government was to employ the traditional tools of trade
policy, tax advantages, pricing mechanisms, and
credit subsidies to increase productivity and to
provide farmers with incomes approximating those of
"comparable" urban occupations. These two objectives were (and are) obviously in tension with one
another: by artificially raising farm incomes, the
government slows the departure of the least productive farmers from the agricultural sector. Nonetheless, the billions of marks which the Bonn government has poured into structural improvements, agricultural marketing, tax subsidies, farmers'
pensions, interest rebates, agricultural research,
rural electrification, subsidies for fuel and
fertilizer, and pest and insect control have helped
German farmers make a vastly more successful accommodation to modern agricultural practices than was
possible in the late years of the Weimar Republic.

These subsidies have not enabled all farmers to
survive the rigors of international competition—
indeed the government has had to promote the consol-
idation of unprofitable small farms—but the unsuccessful farmer now has alternative opportunities
open to him. Unlike his Weimar counterpart, he has
been able to obtain urban employment in the flourishing German economy; his change of professions is
smoothed by government aid, the psychic strain eased
by the prospect of continuing to raise a few
chickens at his rural home while he commutes to his
city job. The contrast with the combined rural and
urban depression of the Weimar era is striking;
urban prosperity now facilitates an abundant flow of
aid to the farmers who remain on their farms and a
cushioned departure for those who give up farming.

The demographic changes and the economic
modernization during the postwar period have
lessened the distinctive character of the local
societies of the marsh, Geest and hill regions. In
Schleswig-Holstein as elsewhere economic progress,
the improvement of transportation and communica-

tions, intermarriage, and common experiences in
schools, universities, and the army have helped to
erode regional differences:

> While at the turn of the century one could
> still be relatively confident about recognizing
> from external appearance whether a farmer came
> from the marsh, the Geest, Angeln, or Fehmarn,
> in recent generations farmers have evolved more
> and more, in both outward appearance and
> internal character, into a homogeneous type,
> the Schleswig-Holstein farmer.[21]

The general trend toward the family farm in all
three natural regions has contributed to this
process; nonetheless, politically important distinctions in the social structure of the regions still
persist and Rudolf Heberle's advice remains useful:

> If one wants to analyze the social conditions
> from which the political atmosphere derives by
> means of making comparisons within the land
> area of Schleswig-Holstein, then it is appro-
> priate to begin with the three great geograph-
> ical regions of marsh, Geest, and hill region.
> The soil conditions, economic patterns, and
> social structure of the rural population within
> these regions are so different from one another
> that a comparison of electoral results then
> permits far-reaching conclusions about the
> factors determining the formation of public
> opinion.[22]

Despite the upheavals of war and the enormous
postwar immigration into Schleswig-Holstein, the
three regions remain distinct enough that they can
still be compared with profit.

The electoral system and the party "system"
have changed far more than has rural society, and
these changes constitute the third major historical
alteration of the rural political environment. In
place of the multiple parties and proportional
representation of the Weimar Republic, there have
emerged two major parties and a complicated voting
system combining direct election, proportional
representation, and a 5 percent threshold clause.
The complaints of leaders of minor parties strongly
suggest that the new electoral system has fostered
the trend toward two-party dominance, in which

classes which formerly voted for different parties
(e.g., Geest farmers and East Holstein estate
owners) have merged under a single banner (in this
case, that of the CDU), thus blurring former political distinctions. This amalgamation of political
forces occurred not at one sudden and irrevocable
moment, but has taken place gradually over the
postwar period, as the electoral results clearly
demonstrate.

Bundestag election results in Schleswig-
Holstein, as in the nation at large, have registered
the growing dominance of the two major parties, as
Table III-4 indicates. In the early fifties, the
CDU in Schleswig-Holstein made the same strong gains
as did the national party, and it experienced the
same modest decline in 1961 and the same subsequent
recovery. In Schleswig-Holstein and in the Federal
Republic the SPD stagnated in the early fifties but
began a steady and sizable advance from the end of
that decade.

An examination of the results of Landtag elections reveals a similar but rather more complicated
picture. In 1947 the SPD in Schleswig-Holstein
obtained 43.8 percent of the vote, a uniquely
successful performance in two respects: At this
time the Schleswig-Holstein SPD commanded the only
"socialist" majority in the western zone, and this
was the only time until 1972 that it enjoyed a
majority. In 1950 both the SPD and the CDU vote
declined sharply with the emergence of the BHE as a
rallying point for refugees. Both of the major
national parties recovered, but the CDU required
several years longer to achieve results in *Land* and
local elections comparable to its successes in
national elections. During this same period the
BHE, DP and SSW attracted larger followings in
Schleswig-Holstein than they did nationally, and
they did even better in *Land* and local elections
than in national elections. What really stands out
in the electoral charts, however, is the increasingly predominant position of the CDU and the SPD at
all levels, first in national elections, then in
Land and in local balloting.

One other bit of evidence confirms the trend
toward two dominant parties. For most postwar elections the *Statistisches Landesamt* in Kiel has
compiled a state-wide 4 percent electoral sample.
For selected communities special ballots are printed
which, when collected and sorted, break down actual

voting behavior by age and sex. These samples have
been carefully refined so as to give the most
"representative" picture possible; they provide the
most accurate information available about voting
patterns. They show that in every election younger
voters have given a greater percentage of their
ballots to the major parties than have their elders,
suggesting that younger voters to a greater extent
than their elders see the SPD-CDU choice as *the*
choice of political alternatives; the tendency of
new generations of voters to concentrate their
ballots increasingly upon the CDU and the SPD
confirms this impression (see Table III-5).

The steady regrouping of voters around two
major parties is of central importance in postwar
politics. Because it is impossible to understand
the position of a contemporary "neo-Nazi" party
without grasping the character and direction of the
present configuration of political forces, a closer
inspection of the development of the political
parties is mandatory. To reveal changes in the
"political atmosphere" and to expose the precarious
status and peculiar problems of a small and newly-
emergent party of the radical right, it is essential
that one trace the origin of the parties, elucidate
the nature of their support, and show, where necessary, the cause of a party's disappearance. By
examining the major parties—the KPD, SPD, CDU, BHE,
SSW, FDP, DP, and SRP—it will be possible to
comprehend the underlying structural constants in
postwar politics, the major electoral trends, and
the fate of marginal political groupings.

Of the parties founded after 1945 only the SPD
and the KPD were direct descendants of Weimar
parties, and the Communists never really got started
in postwar Schleswig-Holstein. The Allies appointed
a few Communists to government posts, but seem to
have set limits to their influence; in Süderdithmarschen the British refused to allow the election
of a Communist as *Landrat*.[23] The KPD never had mass
support in Schleswig-Holstein and the Communists
themselves squandered any remote chance they might
have had; their procedures in Eastern Europe thoroughly inoculated most Germans against Communism.
The refugees, whose social situation theoretically
disposed them to radicalism, repudiated a doctrine
which they associated with the Russian troops who
had driven them from their homes.

Table III-4

Postwar Election Results

| | 1949 | Bundestagswahlen, Federal Republic | | | | | |
		1953	1957	1961	1965	1969	1972
CDU/CSU	31.0	45.2	50.2	45.3	47.6	46.1	44.9
SPD	29.2	28.8	31.8	36.2	39.3	42.7	45.8
FDP	11.9	9.5	7.7	12.8	9.5	5.8	8.4
GDP*	4.0	9.1	8.0	2.8	–	0.1	–
NPD	–	–	–	–	2.0	4.3	.6
Others	23.9	7.3	2.4	2.9	1.6	1.0	.3
Total	100.0	99.9	100.1	100.0	100.0	100.0	100.0

| | 1949 | Bundestagswahlen, Schleswig-Holstein | | | | | |
		1953	1957	1961	1965	1969	1972
CDU	30.7	47.1	48.1	41.8	48.2	46.2	42.0
SPD	29.6	26.5	30.8	36.4	38.8	43.5	48.6
FDP	7.4	4.5	5.6	13.8	9.4	5.2**	8.6
DP	12.1	4.0	3.8	3.9**	–	0.1**	–
BHE	–	11.6	8.3	–	–	–	–
NPD	–	–	–	–	2.4	4.3	–
SSW	5.4	3.3	2.5	1.9	–	–	.5
Others	14.8	3.0	0.8	2.3	1.2	0.6	.3
Total	100.0	100.0	99.9	100.1	100.0	99.9	100.0

Table III-4 (continued)

| | Landtagswahlen, Schleswig-Holstein | | | | | | |
	1947	1950	1954	1958	1962	1967	1971
CDU	34.1	19.8	32.2	44.4	45.0	46.0	51.9
SPD	43.8	27.5	33.2	35.9	39.2	39.4	41.0
FDP	5.0	7.1	7.5	5.4	7.9	5.9	3.8
DP	–	9.6	5.1	2.8	4.2**	–	–
BHE	–	23.4	14.0	6.9	–	–	–
NPD	–	–	–	–	–	5.8	1.3
SSW	9.3	5.5	3.5	2.8	2.3	1.9	1.4
Others	7.9	7.2	4.5	1.8	1.3	0.9	0.7
Total	100.1	100.1	100.0	100.0	99.9	99.9	100.1

* 1949: DP; 1953 and 1957: DP and GB/BHE
** 1961, 1962, and 1969: GDP

Table III-5

Votes According to Sex and Age

	Of 100 Women, ...% voted...				Of 100 Men, ...% voted...			
	CDU	SPD	FDP	BHE	CDU	SPD	FDP	BHE
1953:								
Age 21-30	53	26			47	30		
Age 30-60	50	25			42	29		
Age 60 & over	54	24			46	29		
Average	51	25			44	29		
1957:								
Age 21-30	52	32	5	6	44	38	6	5
Age 30-60	51	29	5	8	42	35	6	8
Age 60 & over	55	25	4	10	45	32	5	10
Average	52	28	5	8	43	35	6	8
1961:								
Age 21-30	44	36	14		39	41	14	3
Age 30-60	43	36	14		36	40	15	4
Age 60 & over	47	33	11		39	39	12	6
Average	44	35	13		37	40	14	4
1962:								
Age 21-30	50.9	36.5	7.2		45.3	41.0	7.4	
Age 30-60	46.4	37.8	8.0		38.5	44.8	8.9	
Age 60 & over	49.5	35.6	7.1		39.8	41.6	8.5	
Average	48.1	36.9	7.6		40.1	43.2	8.5	

Table III-5 (continued)

	Of 100 Women, ...% voted...				Of 100 Men, ...% voted...			
	CDU	SPD	FDP	BHE	CDU	SPD	FDP	BHE
1965:								
Age 21-30	51.8	36.9	8.9		47.7	40.9	8.3	
Age 30-45	48.4	38.3	10.3		39.6	47.0	9.7	
Age 45-60	50.6	36.3	9.6		42.6	41.2	10.8	
Age 60 & over	54.8	34.5	8.1		43.8	41.9	9.9	
Average	51.5	36.4	9.2		43.2	42.9	9.7	
1967:								
Age 21-30	52.8	37.1	5.6		45.7	39.9	6.5	
Age 30-45	48.0	39.4	6.2		37.8	45.9	6.1	
Age 45-60	49.8	36.7	6.1		37.6	42.1	7.4	
Age 60 & over	54.8	35.3	4.6		40.9	42.7	6.1	
Average	51.4	37.0	5.6		40.0	43.0	6.5	

Source: Sonderdienst des Statistischen Landesamtes Schleswig-Holstein 1953: Reihe Wahlen, 7-80-7; Statistische Berichte, 1957, 1961, 1962, 1965, 1967.

The other "successor party," the SPD, had
resolved not to repeat its failures of the Weimar
period; but by failures, the SPD leader, Kurt
Schumacher, understood chiefly the SPD's allowing
the bourgeois parties to steal the national issue.
Under his leadership the party tendentiously
proclaimed its loyalty to the unity of the German
nation[24] and fought a courageous and successful
fight against the Communists; but otherwise the SPD
was the old, tired, unsuccessful party of Weimar
days. The SPD in Schleswig-Holstein won the first
Land election, but failed to break its old class
boundaries, to overcome antiquated dogmas, to purge
itself of its ancient bureaucracy and personnel.
The SPD rejected overtures for the formation of a
"Labor party" and a possible alliance with farm
representatives.[25] It spoke of nationalization and
then repudiated its minister of agriculture when he
proposed a land reform program with real teeth in
it. It filled offices with elderly, incompetent
party hacks incapable of mastering the area's grave
problems.

The magnitude of these problems plus the SPD's
inadequate response to them led to the party's
political decline and fall from office after 1948.
Not until the late 1950s did signs of a revival
become apparent, but then the SPD began to gain
ground steadily on the CDU. Under the leadership of
Jochen Steffen the SPD in Schleswig-Holstein has won
the reputation of being the most leftist section of
the party in the country. "Red Jochen" solicits the
votes of all those who depend upon their own labor
to make a living, but it is not altogether clear
whether his party has made its gains because of or
in spite of his fiery intellectual leadership.

In general the SPD scores its greatest electoral successes in highly urbanized areas (see
Appendix I). In rural areas the CDU customarily
enjoys a two-to-one advantage, but in cities with a
population of more than 50,000 the SPD is the
strongest party. In 1972 the SPD won 54.8 percent
of the vote in such cities, but only 33.1 percent of
the vote in the most rural districts (communities
with less than 250 inhabitants). A glance at an
electoral map confirms this pattern: the SPD does
best in the industrial villages and working-class
communities in and near Kiel, Neumünster, Itzehoe,
and Hamburg. The only exception to this rule is the
East Holstein estate area in the Baltic hill region,

a Social Democratic stronghold since the late 1800s.
Here the SPD obtains a higher percentage of votes in
rural than in urban areas. In rural areas (as, of
course, in urban ones) the SPD draws the bulk of its
support from laborers. The SPD has no monopoly of
the rural working-class vote, however, for while the
entire working class comprises 48.9 percent of the
rural population, the SPD in 1967 won only 32.2
percent of the vote.

Within the three natural regions the SPD vote
and the percentage of rural workers fail to correlate. For the 1967 election the correlation in the
marsh was .05, on the Geest -.24, and in the hill
area -.05; however, if one holds the proportion of
farm proprietors and family workers constant, one
finds a positive correlation of .34 in the hill area
and .15 in the marsh.[26] In his recent dissertation
on electoral politics in Schleswig-Holstein, Heinz
Sahner found significant variations in the size of
these coefficients from district to district. In
Eiderstedt, where farm workers defer to FDP and CDU
notables, the SPD enjoys little success among rural
laborers; Sahner calculated a negative coefficient
of .56 between the SPD vote and the percentage of
farm workers in this district—in Husum the figure
was -.13.[27] In East Holstein, though, Sahner found
a positive coefficient of .67. More recent interviews in this area disclosed that the SPD vote here
comes increasingly from former farm workers, reared
in the Social Democratic tradition, who now commute
to jobs in urban industrial areas. The farm workers
who remain tend to be the more docile employees that
the employer prefers to retain. The safest conclusion that one can draw from this mixed evidence is
that in rural areas the SPD attracts its support
from commuters and farm workers and that it does
best in areas with sharp class distinctions, a
strong Social Democratic tradition, and a highly
unionized agricultural work force—the outstanding
example of these conditions being East Holstein.

The SPD's failure to deal satisfactorily with
the refugee problem led not only to its fall from
power, but also to the formation of a unique party,
the BHE, the *Bund der Heimatvertriebenen und
Entrechteten*. A really new political phenomenon,
the BHE was created by refugees dissatisfied with
the established parties' timid approach to their
problems. One of the BHE leaders, Dr. Alfred Gille,

Table III-6

SPD Vote in Oldenburg 1947-1967

	Land-tagswahl 1947	Bundes-tagswahl 1953	Land-tagswahl 1962	Bundes-tagswahl 1965	Land-tagswahl 1967
Communities over 2,000	49.69	28.49	38.11	37.26	38.88
Communities under 2,000	57.27	35.72	43.88	44.94	46.86

Source: Sahner, *Die NPD in der Landtagswahl 1967 in Schleswig-Holstein*, p. 131.

later explained, "When my party entered political
life, it was stimulated to do so in very large
measure by the embitterment and despair of tens of
thousands of refugee farmers from the east."[28] The
Allies, recognizing the severity of the refugees'
situation and the possibility that the refugees
would raise radical demands, had banned the formation of refugee parties; consequently, many originally entered the "approved" parties, the CDU, FDP,
and the SPD. In 1949 the future chairman of the
BHE, Waldemar Kraft, and some friends ran as independent candidates for the Bundestag to test the
prospects for an independent refugee party once the
ban was lifted. The results were promising, the
Kraft group decided their time had come, and on
January 8, 1950, the party was founded in Kiel.
     The party's history falls into two periods,
with the turning point about 1955:

     In the first period the BHE presented
     itself as a social party with its emphasis upon
     aid for the refugees and their integration into
     the community. In the second period the BHE
     was more the representative of the right of
     self-determination and the right to one's home-
     land, the opponent of any renunciation of
     former German territories; it aimed at a
     peaceful revision of the Yalta and Potsdam
     agreements through which the expellees' land
     and property would be returned and the old
     social structure restored.[29]

In the first phase the BHE was decidedly a party of
refugees and for refugees. Its electoral support
came from refugees. Every study of the BHE electorate in this period has stressed the close correlation between the number of refugees and the number
of BHE voters. The party's general secretary, Hans
Gerd Fröhlich, concluded an analysis of the 1953
Bundestag election with an observation which enjoys
general agreement:

     ...it has been demonstrated quite unambiguously
     that by far the greatest part of our voters are
     in fact expellees. The few votes that we
     received from the indigenous population we can
     leave wholly out of consideration.[30]

The BHE did proportionately better in smaller communities with greater concentrations of refugees;

their numbers, combined with the poorer opportunities in tiny rural settlements, engendered a greater
sense of solidarity.

The BHE also relied on those refugees who were
least integrated—pensioners, farm workers (often
former farmers), those with low incomes, and those
living in rural areas. Franz Neumann, the closest
student of the party, describes the ideal typical
BHE voters as follows: "They were expellees, and,
specifically, older people, who lived in small,
agriculturally oriented communities...and, finally,
belonged to the socially weak groups within the
population."[31] Although the party kept no central
file on its members, an informed estimate suggested
that only 1 or 2 percent of the party's members were
not refugees.[32] The party had an extraordinarily
high ratio of members to voters. In 1953, 21
percent of BHE voters were party members; in Schleswig-Holstein the figure was slightly higher. As a
party of impoverished refugees without interest
group support—the other refugee associations
remained aloof so as not to affect their political
neutrality and thus alienate those of their members
who belonged to other parties—the BHE lacked the
financial resources for modern campaigning and thus
had to rely heavily on its manpower.

The party's policies as well as its composition
stamped it as a refugee party:

> The hard, clearly directed policy that the
> party...pursued gained it the reputation of
> being a pure interest party, a pure expellee
> party, and destroyed many of its successive
> efforts to broaden its base in different direc-
> tions.[33]

In opposition to these policies a number of small
groups formed, bearing titles which expressed their
determination to fight for the interests of the
native population, *Block der Altbürger, Schleswig-
Holsteinische Gemeinschaft, Schleswig-Holsteinische
Wählervereinigung*. The groupings had no importance,
but they served to cement the BHE into its position
as a party of refugees.

The leaders of the BHE had little responsibility to the party membership; they had much leeway
in running the party and they chose to pursue their
constituency's interests with moderation. Kraft
himself "was no revolutionary."[34] He kept the party
in conservative integrative directions, rejecting

socialization and supporting capitalism. He
preferred to join governing coalitions and promote
the refugees' interests from within the government;
in return for supporting government coalitions Kraft
always demanded BHE control of the ministry for
refugees. Neumann sums up the situation nicely:
"Kraft and Oberländer were men of the Restoration,
who sought to fulfill through a policy of strong
reliance on Adenauer and the CDU the understandable
longing of BHE members to become 'bourgeois' once
again."[35]

    This strategy led, however, to the political
extinction of the BHE. Many of the older refugees
never felt at home in the Federal Republic—they
lived out the remainder of their lives in misery
and mental tribulation—but their sons and daughters
eventually found employment, moving if necessary,
and gradually adopted the local dialects and
customs. As they got jobs and made social and
economic gains, they lost the consciousness of being
in a solidaristic refugee community. The more the
refugees assimilated into West German society, the
more they reflected the divisions of that society;
the more the party contributed to the solution of
refugee problems, the more the social differences
and tensions among the refugees divided the party
into potential SPD and CDU supporters.

    Faced with this problem, the leaders of the BHE
began as early as 1952 to try to broaden the basis
of their appeal. In that year the party added
"*Gesamtdeutsche Block*" to its name as an indication
of increased emphasis upon its stand for German
unity. At the same time it appealed to all the
"damaged" (*Geschädigte*) of the war and its after-
math, an appeal which expressed the party's solici-
tude for the troubles of former Nazis—and attracted
some who retained their former Fascistic beliefs and
who saw the BHE's strong national program as an
ideal front for their activities.

    In 1952 and 1953 the Bundestag passed a series
of laws extending assistance to the refugees. The
passage of these laws and the growth of the economy
accelerated the absorption of the refugees and the
demise of the BHE. The party's losses reduced its
influence in the second Adenauer government. These
developments redounded to the benefit of the strong
nationalist clique within the party who were
pressing for a greater emphasis upon an assertive
foreign policy. In 1955 they succeeded in placing

their stamp upon the party, but not without a
struggle for the party leadership which left the
party weak and divided. From now on the party
increasingly adopted slogans and personnel with
radical rightist tinges. By 1957 the party was
condemning all politicians who did not recognize
Germany's 1945 boundaries (i.e., including Memel,
Danzig, and the Sudetenland) as "the politicians of
renunciation" (*Verzichtpolitiker*). In 1958 the BHE
in Schleswig-Holstein split again, leaving former
Nazis and SS men with a strong position in the
party. The old party had lost its *raison d'etre*:
economic growth had taken its voters and the other
parties its program. In 1957 it lost its representation in the Bundestag and in 1962 its last seats
in the Schleswig-Holstein legislature.[36]

The *Südschleswigscher Wählerverband* (SSW)
started earlier and has endured longer than the BHE,
but like the refugee party it enjoyed its heydey
early in the postwar period and has since lost its
significance. The party had its origins in the
despair of 1945. As one of the movement's founders
expressed the feelings of an important segment of
public opinion,

> Our sons, fathers, and brothers have not
> returned and Germany is shattered. Germany
> will never rise again. A terrible disappoint-
> ment and a kind of madness are seizing men.
> This is the end; we are staying out of it; we
> want peace and quiet at last, and peace is to
> be found only in the north [i.e., in annexation
> by Denmark]. Such were the thoughts of many
> people in South Schleswig.[37]

The politics of secession were plausible only in the
area immediately bordering Denmark. There in mid-
1945 a group of citizens, who had not previously
been active in the movement of the Danish minority,
worked to establish a political association (*Südschleswigscher Verein*) independent of the traditional Danish organization (*Slesvigsk Forening*).
In September 1945, this group, together with
representatives of business and labor, petitioned
Field Marshal Montgomery to carry out their
program—an administrative division of Schleswig
from Holstein. Behind this request lay the desire
to escape the consequences of the war and especially

the flood of refugees from the East German provinces; as a part of Denmark the Schleswigers could
ship German refugees further south. The Danish
government recognized the opportunism behind the
call for Danish annexation and stated that it
considered its boundaries firm. Leaders of the SSW
recognized that their adherents had "often purely
materialistic grounds" for joining the pro-Danish
forces,[38] and indeed it was an ironically amusing
but not particularly edifying fact that that part of
Schleswig-Holstein which had cast the highest
percentage of Nazi votes now flocked to the SSW to
escape the consequences of Nazi policy.

Montgomery refused the SSW's request and banned
the formation of the group, but its members went
over to the old Danish organization, captured it,
and used it as the basis of their movement. From
2,500 members in May 1945 the organization grew to
74,000 in 1948.[39] The essence of their political
demands remained separation from Germany, annexation
to Denmark, and the exclusion of refugees. The
appeal of this program, like that of the BHE's,
presumed economic and psychological distress. As
the German press became active again and began to
denounce the separatists, and as the economy revived,
most of those Germans who elected to cast their lot
with the Danes now reconsidered and, faithful to
their tradition of opportunism, decided that the
grass was greener on the German side of the fence
after all.

The SSW's electoral stronghold has always been
Flensburg; the party has never elicited much
response in small farming communities, except in
North Friesland, an area with sizable Danish
minority and poor economic conditions. Gerhard
Isbary, the leading authority on the SSW phenomenon,
estimates that only 40 percent of native rural
Schleswigers voted SSW as against about 70 percent
of the native urban population.[40] Isbary argues
that the SSW vote was not—with the exception of the
old minorities in Flensburg and a few other communities—a confession of nationality, but

It is to be seen much more as a reflex action
of hungry, insecure, disappointed sectors of
the population, people who linked their vote
with a hope of alleviating their elemental
distress.[41]

The SSW vote in the early postwar years far exceeded
the number of Danish speakers in the 1950 census
(5,991), the number of Danish speakers revealed in a
1936 study, and the Danish vote in the 1920 refer-
endum and in the Weimar elections (12,800 the
highest). All these traditional measures of
"Danishness" cannot account for the SSW's success.

        What does explain it is the despair of the
native population (the refugees voted for the German
parties), the well-organized relief services run by
the Danish, and the desire to exclude the refugees.
The SSW offered an alternative to radicalism:
secession was an alternative to the social restructuring necessary to accommodate the refugees. As
postwar misery gave way to economic revival, the SSW
lost its appeal. Isbary shows in great detail how
the return to the German parties occurred much more
slowly in communities with severe social and
economic problems. In short, the great proportion
of the Danish vote represented the reaction of the
indigenous population to a general crisis; as this
crisis passed, these people once again gave their
votes to German parties, but the speed of this
return varied with the severity of local problems.

        The founders of the dominant bourgeois party,
the *Christlich Demokratische Union* or CDU, sought to
remove the chances for opportunistic enticement of
essentially conservative voters by parties like the
BHE and the SSW. They aimed at the construction of
an "alliance of all forces to the right of Social
Democracy," an aspiration which accorded with the
Allies' desire to promote a three-party system (CDU,
SPD, and KPD) that would prevent the growth of
splinter parties.[42]

        In 1945, as political parties began to form
        once again in North Germany, the groups "to the
        right of Social Democracy" generally pursued
        the goal of preventing the recurrence of the
        splintered party system of Weimar; instead they
        tried to create through an alliance movement a
        two or three party system and a sufficiently
        strong "bourgeois" counterweight to the "Left"
        parties.[43]

This general desire for unity did not exclude the
appearance of different ideological currents. In
Schleswig-Holstein the CDU grew from three main
centers, Plön, Kiel, and Rendsburg. Other indepen-

dent units sprang up in Lübeck and Itzehoe and
various groups forged links with the CDU in Hamburg
(in which "the notables of Hanseatic society gath-
ered"[44]), but the Plön, Kiel, and Rendsburg groups
represented the three major ideological directions
in the party.

The Plön group assembled around the former DNVP
minister, Hans Schlange-Schöningen. Schlange-
Schöningen and his friends came from the landed
elite of eastern Germany, but in postwar categories
they were refugees. They advocated the formation of
a conservative party with a wider basis than the
DNVP; they urged a rally of DNVP, DVP, and DDP
elements on a "Christian" basis. The English Conservative party appealed to them: it was in their eyes
civilized; it was antisocialist; it was bent on
ruling. These qualities largely comprised the sub-
stance of their "Christian-conservative" program.

The Kiel contingent similarly urged the formation of an inclusive bourgeois democratic party, but
its key figures came from the urban liberal rather
than from the agrarian conservative tradition. The
party chairman, Carl Schröter, had been chairman of
the DVP until 1933. Now he reassembled the Kiel
bourgeoisie, bankers, industrialists, teachers,
professors, and pastors. These were men who celebrated the achievements of liberal individualistic
capitalism; they argued against the separation of
church and state, and they rejected "doctrine" in
favor of "experience."[45] Schröter's opponent within
the party, Theodor Steltzer, a participant in the
1944 conspiracy against Hitler and the first postwar
Oberpräsident of Schleswig-Holstein, neatly summarized the position of the Kiel group:

> The Kiel group advocated in a rather simple
> fashion the bourgeois idealism of the National
> Liberals. They wanted to build up the state
> on the basis of an ideologically enlightened
> bourgeoisie...which, however, no longer
> existed.[46]

In Plön the conservatives longed for a nonexistent
ordered hierarchic rural society; in Kiel they
dreamed of an urban society which had disappeared
before 1914. Neither program bore much relevance to
existing structures and problems.

The Rendsburg program was more interesting, but
it too rested on an anachronistic conception, the
liberalism of the Prussian Reform bureaucrats.

Steltzer was the chief architect of this program and
it reflects his great decency and humanity; regret-
tably one must add that it also reflects his vague-
ness about its institutional arrangements.

> The Rendsburg group took a critical stand
> toward both the bourgeois and the socialist
> ideology of the past. It strove for an organic
> arrangement from below in a new ordering of the
> relations of Germany to its constituent states
> and in a transformation of our social relations.
> It wanted to replace the old upper class's
> humanistic ideal of culture and education with
> an essentially broader based educational
> effort.[47]

Here was a praiseworthy recognition that the old
order had passed; to it Steltzer added social
convictions and a willingness to work with the SPD,
but his central appeal for more self-administration
was an inadequate prescription. Steltzer saw solutions arising naturally out of social conflicts and
refused to see the opposed interests behind these
conflicts. Nonetheless, the shortcomings in his
program are those of any conservative program; his
was far more decent than most and certainly the most
humane in the CDU in Schleswig-Holstein. He recognized the moral bankruptcy of Adenauer's program and
he fought the conservative nationalism which grew
increasingly dominant in his party.
    The superiority of the Rendsburg program made
little difference in the long run. At first
Steltzer's influence as *Oberpräsident* assured the
Rendsburg group a dominant position in the party;
but his segment of the party lacked the organizational basis with which to consolidate its grip on
the party, whereas the Kiel group could devote far
more time to party tasks than either Steltzer or
Schlange-Schöningen, both of whom held important
governmental offices. Under Schröter's leadership
the CDU in Schleswig-Holstein became one of the
most conservative and nationalistic branches of
the CDU in the Bundesrepublik. The party's social
basis made this course easier than in other areas of
the Bundesrepublik, for in Protestant Schleswig-
Holstein the party had a negligible number of Catholic working-class supporters. Schröter exploited
bourgeois fears of the SPD and once again unleashed
nationalist emotions, this time against the Danes.

In one *Landtag* speech he called Danish policy "impe-
rialist, aggressive, and inhumane," surely one of
the most repulsive and tasteless utterances by any
postwar German politician.[48]

The CDU's strongly nationalist and conservative
rhetoric certainly did not harm the party in rural
Schleswig-Holstein. The CDU has traditionally
polled almost twice as many votes as the SPD in
rural areas; the 1972 statistics disclosed that 59.6
percent of voters in communities with fewer than 250
inhabitants cast their ballots for the CDU (as
opposed to only 35.4 percent of the voters in cities
over 100,000). The generalization that the smaller
the community the larger the CDU vote and the
smaller the SPD vote has become increasingly accurate. Although the CDU and the SPD have both gained
new adherents in communities of all sizes since the
early postwar elections, the CDU has made its
greatest relative gains in small rural communities.[49]

In a recent study of the political ecology of
Schleswig-Holstein, Heinz Sahner found remarkably
high correlations (from +.55 to +.74) between the
CDU vote in 1967 and the NSDAP vote in 1930-1933.
His conclusion is incontrovertible: "Today the CDU
in Schleswig-Holstein has the same ecological
concentrations as the NSDAP in the thirties."[50]
Like the NSDAP, the CDU has dominated the rural
family farming areas. The farmers' adherence to the
CDU is no accident; the party has courted the
farmers with singular intensity. No other interest
group has received such consistent attention and
support in CDU platforms and policies. In this
connection the contribution of Bundestag representative Detlef Struve, a Rendsburg farmer and with
Steltzer a cofounder of the Rendsburg CDU group, in
enlisting rural support for the CDU cannot be overestimated. As Adenauer's trusted adviser on farm
policy, this long-time officeholder won important
concessions for farmers all over West Germany, not
merely for those in Schleswig-Holstein. His efforts
have cemented the attachment of his local rural
constituents to the CDU.

Ecological electoral analysis demonstrates this
intimate connection between the CDU and the family
farmers. The CDU draws its strongest support from
the Geest; there the party's vote averages five to
eight percentage points higher than in the marshes
or hill area (see Appendix II). These CDU successes
reflect differences in social structure: the Geest

has a slightly higher proportion of people employed
in agriculture than do the other two regions;
furthermore, within the agricultural sector the
percentage of independent proprietors and their
family helpers is greatest on the Geest (see Table
III-7). The hills, on the other hand, have a much
higher proportion of dependent employees on their
farms. The electoral results correlate with these
differences. The CDU dominates the Geest area, the
region of family farming, and the SPD does best in
the hill area, the center of large-scale manorial
agriculture. Within regions the CDU also does best
where the family farm predominates; for example
within the hill area the CDU piles up its heaviest
vote among Angeln's family farmers, does less well
in the mixed estate and farm territory of Eckernförde, and declines still further in the manorial
districts of Plön and Oldenburg.

     Such public opinion poll data as are available
confirm the CDU's strong electoral base among rural
proprietors. Unfortunately, no really dependable
surveys of public opinion in Schleswig-Holstein yet
exist. National surveys do not select enough
participants to yield reliable results at the *Land*
level. The University of Kiel conducted a survey
in 1955, but the technique of sending out question-
naires and requesting replies resulted in an inadequate sample, prone to bias. The farmers who did
answer the questionnaire indicated a strong preference for the CDU. Similarly material from the data
pool at the University of Köln revealed that from a
sample of twenty-two farmers surveyed in 1966, eight
of the twelve who expressed a party preference chose
the CDU, two chose the FDP, and one each the SPD and
the NPD.[51] Such minute samples hardly permit generalization, but it would be foolish to deny the
strong attachment of Schleswig-Holstein farmers to
the CDU. No other social bloc votes so decidedly
for a particular party.[52]

     The great similarity of economic interests in
small rural communities and the fact that the CDU
champions these interests while the SPD does not,
largely explain the overwhelming CDU majorities in
these areas; but tighter social controls also play
a role. The farmer who depends upon the local co-
operative (customarily dominated by CDU "notables")
for an essential loan will be reluctant to advertise
himself as an SPD partisan—nor does the SPD offer
him much incentive to do so. The CDU's party orga-

Table III-7

*Persons Employed in Agriculture and Forestry
in the Three Natural Regions
(Communities under 2,000 Inhabitants)*

	Marsh (%)	Geest (%)	Hill Area (%)
Independent Proprietors	14.94	15.26	11.46
Family Help	19.52	22.66	15.46
Dependent Farm Workers	7.78	8.87	15.30

Source: *Gemeindestatistik von Schleswig-Holstein
1960/61.*

nization, originally almost nonexistent in rural
areas, has expanded and become increasingly effective. No longer do the old *Rathausparteien*, the
informal bourgeois coalitions assembled for local
elections, dominate rural politics between national
elections; the structure of local politics has been
"modernized." Although some tension persists
between rural notables who wish to remain "above
parties" and CDU managers who want party discipline,
the CDU has succeeded in capturing the old local
coalitions through a combination of legal measures
and political favors. The CDU has "politicized"
rural local government; it has organized the
villages under its banner.[53]

In 1945 and 1946 the proper name for the new
bourgeois party was a topic of considerable contro-
versy. For various reasons many hesitated to append
the name "Christian" to the party; the crux of the
matter was that a number of former liberals
preferred to avoid any weakening of the traditional
liberal positions against state intervention on
behalf of the church or the working class. When in
Rendsburg on January 4, 1946, the new bourgeois
party was officially founded, it adopted the name
"Democratic Union." As the party took up ties with
the national CDU in mid-February, a faction led by
industrialists from Itzehoe split off in protest and
formed the FDP.
    The Allies recognized the *Freie Demokratische
Partei* in May 1946, but this splinter group never

succeeded in recapturing a body of supporters
comparable to the former DVP and DDP. The electoral
statistics for the FDP reflect its change first from
a party of the small-town bourgeoisie to a party of
rural "notables," and then its more recent evolution
into an urban reform party (see Appendix I). The
FDP has made its best electoral showing in the
marshes and particularly in Eiderstedt, where its
most distinguished candidates have lived. In remote
Eiderstedt personal friendship and esteem as well as
the traditional mechanisms of deference play a most
important role; in 1967 the FDP vote yielded a positive coefficient of .51 with the percentage of farm
workers. This evidence reaffirms the point that the
FDP remained—at least until 1969—a liberal *Honor-
atiorenpartei*, a party which survived the inner-
party factionalism of the 1950s by delicate compromise and finally went over to Scheel's progressive
course in the late 1960s—but at the cost of losing
some of its "notables" and, with them, a significant
part of the party's membership.

Still further to the right than the CDU and FDP
was the German Party (*Deutsche Partei* or DP). The
DP began in Lower Saxony (Niedersachsen) as the
anachronistic successor to the old Guelph party and
its predecessor, the *Deutsch-Hannoverische Partei*.[54]
It originally advocated the establishment of an
independent Lower Saxony and the dissolution of
Prussia. The fulfillment of these demands in 1946
and 1947 eliminated the rationale for its existence
as a regional party and the party responded by
attempting to broaden itself. From 1947 to 1949 it
spread throughout the British zone; from late 1949
it expanded into the rest of the Federal Republic.
It espoused a conservative nationalist program,
stressing the concerns of agriculture and of the
most conservative sections of the bourgeoisie, but
it never clearly distinguished itself from CDU or
the radical rightist parties. Up through 1953 it
maintained a calculated ambiguity toward the NSDAP,
campaigned openly for former Nazis, and asked recognition of the honor of the "pure soldiery." "Who-
ever sullies the honor of German soldiers is to be
punished."[55]
These tactics did not prevent its participating
in the governing coalition and claiming credit for
all of the successes and none of the failures of the
Adenauer regime. It is pleasant to be able to

record that these tactics were unsuccessful. Hell-
wege, the party chairman, recognized this fact;
following the 1953 election he wrote that "the
utilization of 'erstwhiles' [former Nazis] and of
the black-white-red colors for the sake of tactical
successes we shall have to give up in the future.
It hurts more than it helps."[56] After this election
the DP emphasized its conservatism rather than its
nationalism—with an equal lack of success.

     Students of the DP, while not concealing reac-
tionary and Fascistic trends within the party, have
stopped short of applying these terms to the party
as a whole. This conclusion strikes this writer as
highly dubious and particularly so for Schleswig-
Holstein. When the party organization in *Kreis*
Eckernförde dissolved itself, all but two members
announced their switch to the neo-Nazi SRP. When
the party expelled a prominent member for pro-Nazi
and anti-Semitic utterances, no less than five *Kreis*
organizations left the party with him. These cases
leave little doubt that the DP in Schleswig-Holstein
harbored a sizable number of incorrigible Nazis.
This is not to say that the DP in Schleswig-Holstein
was a neo-Nazi party; neo-Nazi elements were prominent, but not predominant. The problem of distinguishing conservatism from reaction and Fascism is
seldom easy, and the DP did little to make the
distinctions clear.

     The existence of an SPD government in Schleswig-
Holstein from 1947 until 1950 provided an incentive
for the bourgeois parties to unify themselves, and
in 1950 proposals for a unified conservative front
reemerged. The *Union im Norden*, the organ of the
CDU in Schleswig-Holstein, demanded the merger of
CDU, FDP, and DP into a "German Bloc." The three
parties contracted an electoral alliance for the
1950 *Landtag* elections, and in some local districts
preparations for a definitive merger were laid,[57]
but the Bloc's poor showing in the elections dashed
hopes for a single inclusive right-wing party. The
smaller parties discussed amalgamation as they lost
voters, but the trend toward a two-party system
resulted more from the movement of voters than from
the action of parties. The DP, after unsuccessful
talks with the FDP, engaged in a marriage of conve-
nience with the BHE in 1960-61, but this union was
the final fling of two old rejected parties.

     Parties on the extreme right have had trouble
organizing in postwar Germany. First the Allies

flatly prohibited such formations, giving the
"approved" parties a four or five year head start,
and then from 1951 the German Constitutional Court
held the threat of dissolution over antidemocratic
parties. In the brief period between the end of
Allied licensing of political parties (March 30,
1950 in the British zone) and the beginning of the
functioning of the Constitutional Court (September
1951), a number of small radical right-wing movements emerged. Of these new extremist factions the
most important was the *Sozialistische Reichspartei*
(SRP), an amalgam of radical nationalists who had
split off from the DP and from small ultra-rightist
factions like the DRP, DKP, and NDP.[58]

   In its politics the SRP proceeded from a peculiar conception of the existing situation; namely,
that the Third Reich, with Admiral Dönitz as legitimate head of state, continued to exist! From this
starting point the party derived the conclusion that
the Bundesrepublik constituted an illegal and ille-
gitimate state structure. The SRP persevered in a
vengeful "front consciousness" (*"Frontbewusstsein"*)
and represented the German people as still carrying
on a struggle for the realization of its war aims.
From the idea of the illegality and illegitimacy of
the West German Republic the party inferred a right
of permanent resistance to the democratic state. To
this *"Widerstandsrecht"* they added a missionary
consciousness and dedicated themselves to the reconstruction of the *"Reich"* and the restructuring of
the German *"Volk"* into a *"führungsdemokratische
völkische Gemeinschaft."* The SRP conceived its
mission as forging together the *"frontbewusste"* and
"reichstreue" *"Elite"* of the German people into a
political order which would then lead the transition
from a *"Volksgemeinschaft"* to a *"Tatgemeinschaft."*
To their tasks the new elitist clique must bring
unconditional subordination to the party leadership,
"Kameradschaft," and a conception of the solidarity
of the "order." "The SRP apologists did not deny
the rooting of their ideology in National Socialism."[59] The party termed itself the heir of the
National Socialist revolution. National Socialist
terms such as *"artgebundene Volksgemeinschaft,"*
"volklich gebundener Sozialismus", and similarly
elusive expressions were constantly used. What
democratic rhetoric the party employed served to
camouflage its unconstitutional character rather
than to specify its true ambitions.

The party's base lay in Niedersachsen and from there the party spread to Schleswig-Holstein in April 1950, picking Rendsburg as its center. At this point the party had established only a few small beachheads. The party gradually expanded its network over the entire *Land*, partly by setting up its own local apparatus, partly by winning over former DRP supporters. In *Kreis* Eckernförde a renegade DP member had founded a branch. For the *Landtag* elections of July 1950, the party put on a burst of organizational activity and on the date of the election the leader of this effort reported "strong local organizations" in all but three *Kreisen*; "strong" seems to have meant a membership of 50 to 100, for available evidence points to units of this size.[60] The largest local organizations consisted chiefly of unemployed; men out of work made up 65 percent of the Stormarn and Süderdith-marschen units and the party archives revealed that the Lauenburg organization, too, was composed of "predominantly unemployed"[61]—facts which suggest the possibility of members' mellowing later through participation in the economic boom.

An analysis of the party's electorate in Schleswig-Holstein cannot be very reliable, because the party's total vote (1.6 percent) was small and because an alteration of the electoral law five days before the election caused the party to change its whole electoral strategy. Previously the large number of signatures necessary to place direct candidates on the ballot had led the SRP to urge its supporters to vote for the bourgeois coalition ticket; when the new law allowed them to put on more candidates, they urged that voters now choose the party itself. "With this tactic the party, on the eve of the election, confused its constituency completely."[62] This confusion suggests that the final vote may not have accurately reflected the SRP's appeal.[63] Following the election the party continued its organizational activity and did succeed in recruiting new members. Lauenburg and Süderdithmarschen provided the strongest contingents with 75 to 100 members; in *Kreis* Schleswig the party attracted 50 to 75 members; in Neumünster, Lübeck, Stormarn, and Oldenburg 25 to 50. All of the remaining units had less than 25 members.[64]

On the twenty-third of October, 1953, the Constitutional Court put an end to the SRP's activity. The Court rested its ban on four major

conclusions: (1) that the SRP promoted anti-
Semitism and disregarded human rights; (2) that it
opposed the existing parties in a manner that demonstrated that it was against a multi-party system;
(3) that the party's internal organization was
totalitarian; and (4) that in program, conceptions,
style, and in part in personnel, the party was
Nazistic.   These conclusions rested in turn on
expert testimony stressing the links between the SRP
and the Nazis.   The Court's decision certified the
party's demise.   Vigorous enforcement of the ruling,
especially in Lower Saxony, eliminated successor
groups as soon as they were formed.   It is important
to observe, however, that social, economic, and
administrative pressure alone did not defeat the
SRP.

> Neither the educational work of democratic
> propaganda nor the hindrance of SRP agitation
> through disruption of their meetings and
> speeches and through prohibition of their meet-
> ings nor the measures of the Federal Government
> sufficed to put a stop to the gradual organiza-
> tional strengthening of the party.[65]

Legal measures were necessary.   They did succeed.
They did act as a deterrent and constraint to future
organized party activity by neo-Nazi organizations.

In order to understand the present political
situation and its dominant lines of development it
is necessary to observe the changes in the political
infrastructure discussed in this chapter—the influx
and gradual assimilation of the refugees and expellees, the decline of the agricultural sector and the
concomitant modernization of farming operations, the
steady elimination of minor parties, and the gradual
emergence of two dominant parties.   To fully appreciate the situation that the NPD faced in the late
1960s, however, one has to take into account the
long-term growth of the SPD and the relative stagna-
tion of the CDU (see Table III-4 and Appendix I).
From a dismal low in 1953, when it obtained
only 26.5 percent of the vote, the SPD in Schleswig-
Holstein has steadily increased its share of the
vote until (in 1972) it succeeded in breaking, at
least temporarily, the CDU's long domination.   The
CDU vote over the same period shows occasional
upward fluctuations, but on the whole the party's

share of the vote in *Land* and national elections has
remained around 46 to 47 percent; it has improved
its position most in communities with under 2,000
inhabitants—the declining rural villages. The SPD
leader, Jochen Steffen, has not hesitated to portray
the CDU as the captive of a disappearing minority
(viz., the farmers) which shapes CDU policy in ways
inimical to the interests of a majority of the population. This argument, partisan though it may be,
contains considerable truth. The CDU in the late
1960s was an elderly party tied to disappearing
classes and largely dependent upon the "watering
can" (*Giesskanne*) system of patronage and electoral
favors for its success; the party's principles
extended little farther than nationalism and opposition to socialism. If the party were to move to the
left, it had to fear NPD inroads among its rural
clientele; if it did not move to the left, it
exposed itself to continued SPD gains. This crisis
in the affairs of the ruling party and the concomitant challenge by the NPD and the SPD presented the
most interesting and potentially the most dangerous
political situation in the postwar period.

4: The NPD in Electoral Politics

Any comparison of political phenomena, whether transnational or transtemporal, involves annoying and embarrassing questions about the feasibility or even the possibility of comparison. Just what is the basis of comparison? Wolfgang Hirsch-Weber and Klaus Schütz in their study of the Federal elections of 1953, *Wähler und Gewählte*, argue that a study like the present one, comparing electoral results before and after Nazism, is not really practicable.

> The experience of National Socialist policies and their consequences, of war, and of total collapse have put the political decisions of individuals in the postwar period on a basis which is hardly comparable with the Weimar period. If it is possible at all to generate categories for a comparative analysis that extends back before 1933, then these categories must be provided by social psychology rather than by a political science oriented to statistical data.[1]

Although the historical electoral studies of Günther Franz and of the Institut für vergleichende Sozialforschung in Germany, Francois Goguel in France, Perry Howard in America, and numerous others would seem to belie this conclusion, it may be useful to consider briefly the case against such comparisons.[2]
Hirsch-Weber and Schütz make three arguments: (1) The parties before 1933 and those after 1945 are

too dissimilar to be compared; (2) the populations are too dissimilar to be compared; and (3) the twelve-year National Socialist regime represents too long a period of suppression of free elections to make reliable comparisons possible. To the first argument the reply is that even parties with the same name differ from one election to the next and that, furthermore, what is of interest is the *tendance* of parties or groups of parties, the similarity of their ideologies and support. Such similarity can be discovered (if it exists at all) only be careful empirical investigation in each case. To the second argument chapter three should serve as both a concession and a reply: the influx of refugees has created great but not insuperable problems for comparative study, for the refugees have not reconstructed Schleswig-Holstein society, but been absorbed into it. The point of the third argument is not altogether clear. Length of time alone does not seem to be the crucial factor prohibiting comparisons; Hirsch-Weber and Schütz themselves compare data extending over a seven-year period.

In any case—and this argument is the crucial one—no one can make an *a priori* judgment about the utility of such transtemporal comparisons; one has to survey the relevant data, attempt the comparisons, and see whether they are enlightening. That is the procedure employed in this analysis of NPD and NSDAP voting. This chapter briefly sketches the electoral history and the political stance of the NPD in Schleswig-Holstein and then, following the precedent of chapters two and three, attempts to ascertain on the basis of the available evidence just who supports the NPD and why. The analysis naturally leads into a discussion of the factors limiting the NPD's electoral prospects. A more detailed comparison of the reasons for Nazi success and neo-Nazi failure is reserved for the final chapter.

The NPD in Schleswig-Holstein was founded in 1964 and made its first major electoral effort in the national elections of 1965. The newly-formed party, a diverse assemblage of experienced nationalist politicians and political novices bent on becoming the "national opposition," did best in Oldenburg, the home territory of one of its future *Landtag* representatives, Uwe Rheingans. In Oldenburg the NPD drew 3.9 percent of the vote, well above the 2.4 percent it received in Schleswig-

Holstein as a whole. In ensuing years the party retained its base in Oldenburg and made significant inroads on the west coast.

Norder- and Süderdithmarschen gave the NPD 7.6 percent and 7.4 percent of ballots cast for *Landtag* delegates in 1967—percentages topped only by Oldenburg's 8.2 percent. Throughout Schleswig-Holstein the party collected 5.8 percent of the vote, enough to surmount the 5 percent clause and to send four representatives into the Schleswig-Holstein *Landtag*; in addition to Rheingans, Peter Petersen, the party's agricultural spokesman, Karl-Ernst Lober, the party chairman from Schleswig, and Wolfgang Ehlers, a Dithmarschen farmer, entered the new assembly.

Two years later, in the Bundestag elections of 1969, the party lost ground in every *Kreis* and managed to obtain only 4.3 percent of the vote. The party lost just over 9,000 voters, getting 62,912 ballots instead of 72,093. By the 1972 Bundestag election the NPD, once deemed a serious threat to political stability in West Germany, could not garner even 1 percent of the vote in Schleswig-Holstein.

If one asks why the NPD should have emerged as a serious competitor to the established parties when it did, a flippant but largely accurate answer is that it was formed then. Parties of the nationalist right had always attracted votes in the postwar period, and when the NPD arose as a union of these forces, it collected votes which had formerly gone to these parties. Foremost among these was the GDP, for which Peter Petersen also acted as a radically reactionary agricultural spokesman. Sahner has noted a significant correlation between the vote for the NPD and the vote for its predecessors (see Table IV-1). These data and some continuity in personnel between the NPD and its predecessors strongly suggest the persistence of a small group of politicians and voters imbued with sentiments so conservative and so nationalistic that they cannot be satisfied by the CDU in Schleswig-Holstein. This analysis, however, does not constitute an adequate answer to the question of why the NPD should have suddenly blossomed as a distinctly menacing political force in 1967.

The NPD's largest percentage gains in 1967 came in rural Schleswig-Holstein. To some extent these gains reflected general disenchantment with the

Table IV-1

Correlations between NPD Vote and the Vote
of Some Other Rightist Parties
in the Postwar Period

	GDP 1962	GDP 1961	DRP 1953
NPD 1967 (n=21 *Kreise*)	.57	.61	.48

Source: Sahner, *Politische Tradition, Sozial-*
struktur und Parteiensystem in Schleswig-
Holstein, p. 32.

political system and the "Great Coalition" of the
CDU and SPD in particular. These motives have been
sufficiently analyzed elsewhere, and need not be
detailed here, particularly since there is little
indication that they prompted large numbers of rural
voters to switch allegiances. What was decisive for
these sudden electoral gains was downward pressure
on farm incomes, which farmers traced to the effects
of German participation in the European community's
common agricultural policy.

The CDU simply had not foreseen the possibility
of agricultural surpluses within the Common Market,
and hence did not prepare farmers psychologically or
technically for the intensified competition they
faced.[3] The farmers' interest organization, the
Bauernverband, was equally unperceptive. When farm
prices failed to keep pace with increases in farm
costs (from December 1966 to August 1967 farmers
watched the prices of their products drop 9 percent
while their costs continued to rise),[4] the *Bauern-*
verband took the offensive against the European
Economic Community (EEC). The CDU, conscious of its
international position, did not enjoy the same flex-
ibility; it had to appeal for farmers' support on
the basis of its previous successes, thus allowing
the NPD to raise that traditional political question,
"What have you done for me lately?" The NPD, bearing no political responsibilities, could call for
large farm subsidies; the CDU, with forebodings of
the consequences of building its political future on
a declining class, needed to preserve budgetary
resources to be able to dole out favors to other

political groups. The result of all these pressures—of declining margins on farm products, of
increasing dissatisfaction with the EEC and with the
party that took German farmers into the Common
Market—was a substantial disenchantment with CDU
agricultural policy and a political opening for the
NPD.

The NPD in Schleswig-Holstein moved to exploit
this opening with campaign propaganda that was
considerably more moderate than that of the NPD's
national organ, the *Deutsche Nachrichten*. NPD
spokesmen sounded two major themes: the desir-
ability of a truly German foreign policy and the
necessity of aid for embattled sections of the
middle class. The party courted farmers with
particular zeal; in the *Landtag* about two-thirds of
their early motions and bills were aimed at
providing higher prices for farm products and more
aid for struggling farmers.[5] In general the party
tried to present an image of sobriety and responsibility. In Ahrensburg an NPD spokesman took pains
to distance himself from the national party's use of
expressions reminiscent of the late 1920s, "*Blut und
Boden*," "*Asphaltliteratur*," "*Ungeist dieser Zeit
überwinden*," and the like.[6] At its annual convention in 1968 the party laid claim to the title
"protectress of the democratic legal state"
("*Hüterin des demokratischen Rechtstaates*"),
contending that the NPD was neither authoritarian,
ultranationalistic, nor war-seeking.[7] A former Nazi
Gauleiter, somewhat contemptuous of these pacifica-
tory gestures, termed the NPD a "bourgeois club...
without ideas."[8]

The party did contain former Nazis, but they
played no appreciable role in the leadership of the
Land party: of sixteen leading candidates in the
1969 Bundestag elections, only four were former
Nazis, and of these, three had joined in 1941 or
later. Hans Kehr, the chief of the NPD *Ordnungs-
dienst*, had easily the worst record among the party
elite; a former SA and SS man, Kehr after 1945
served four years for beatings he inflicted in
1934.[9] In building up its organization the party
consulted former Nazi leaders, but enlisted very
few.

The party's propaganda occasionally dropped
strong hints for the titillation of former Nazis,
but its spokesmen generally chose their words carefully. A Flensburg paper reported a Rheingans
speech as follows:

The national [idea] was for him and his party
the decisive motive power in politics; he
plainly confessed his dedication to the
hallowed national tradition. The German Reich
had twice been overpowered and defeated by its
enemies; the violent solutions (*Gewaltlösungen*)
of 1945 must be revised without fail; the
renunciation of the German eastern territories
constituted a total capitulation....[10]
[Rheingans made these remarks before a group of
young Jews from London.]

Nationalistic outbursts, professions of admiration
for military figures and institutions, repeated
calls for amnesty for war criminals, and protests
against American and Soviet domination all offered
publicists opportunity to brand the NPD as a neo-
Nazi party. The party's political opponents
welcomed and fostered this interpretation, but a
dispassionate survey of the evidence leads to the
conclusion that the NPD is not a neo-Nazi party.
Nationalistic, yes; reactionary, yes; but the
Schleswig-Holstein branch of the NPD is neither an
overtly racist nor a totalitarian party: it is the
ideological successor of the DNVP, not the NSDAP.
    For the present purpose what the NPD in
Schleswig-Holstein is (the ideological successor of
the DNVP) is less important than what it is
perceived to be (a neo-Nazi party). NPD leaders
cite the image of their party as one of their
greatest obstacles, and the overwhelming majority of
the electorate automatically treat the NPD as the
contemporary version of the Nazi party, condemning
or praising it accordingly. Thus for the purpose of
this investigation the ideological differences are
unimportant; most people believe the NPD to be a
neo-Nazi party and support or reject it on those
grounds.
    Four kinds of evidence help to identify who
the NPD's voters are: the *Statistisches Landesamt*'s
4 percent sample of actual ballots, ecological analysis of voting results, public opinion polls, and
interviews. The 4 percent representative samples
yield the data in Table IV-2. The figures show
clearly and incontrovertibly (1) that the NPD
exerts a greater attraction for men than for women,
and (2) that the NPD appeals most to the 45-60 age
group among both men and women, people who were born
between 1905 and 1924 and who were between 9 and 28
years old when the Nazis came to power. This group

Table IV-2

NPD Vote According to Sex and Age

Of 1,000 Men, ...% voted NPD	Bundestagswahl	Landtagswahl	Bundestagswahl	Landtagswahl
Ages	*1965*	*1967*	*1969*	*1971*
21–30	2.1	5.8	3.8	--
30–45	2.3	7.6	5.1	--
45–60	3.5	10.3	8.6	--
60 and over	2.8	7.6	6.2	--
Average	2.7	8.0	6.0	2.0

Of 1,000 Women, ...% voted NPD	Bundestagswahl	Landtagswahl	Bundestagswahl	Landtagswahl
Ages	*1965*	*1967*	*1969*	*1971*
21–30	1.1	2.8	--	--
30–45	1.8	4.2	2.7	--
45–60	2.5	5.2	4.0	--
60 and over	1.6	3.2	2.6	--
Average	1.8	4.0	2.8	1.0

Source: Statistische Berichte, 1965, 1967, 1969, 1971.

(By 1972 the NPD was so small that the Statistisches Landesamt did not bother to publish similar calculations.)

may contain many early Nazis, but women and *alte Kämpfer* are not a major source of NPD strength; they constitute only a small percentage of the NPD electorate.

The second type of evidence, ecological analysis, is somewhat less enlightening, since the low percentage of votes obtained by the NPD makes such analysis rather inconclusive. The analysis of results by community size does show that since 1965 the NPD has been more successful in smaller communities (see Table IV-3). The NPD's appeal clearly wanes in urban areas. If one examines the geographical distribution of the NPD vote, one obtains further confirmation of this point; Dithmarschen, Oldenburg, the area west of Preetz, and portions of Lauenburg show concentrations of NPD voters, but the larger cities—Lübeck, Kiel, Flensburg, and Rendsburg—do not (see Appendix III and Map 3).

The Nazis also achieved greater successes in rural than in urban areas and they too turned Dith-

Table IV-3

NPD Vote by Size of Community

	BTW 1965	LTW 1967	BTW 1969	LTW 1971	BTW 1972
Under 250	2.6	8.9	8.2	2.7	.9
250-500	2.1	7.7	6.6	2.1	.8
500-750	2.2	7.4	6.1	1.9	.7
750-1,000	2.2	6.8	5.4	1.7	.6
1,000-2,000	2.2	6.4	4.9	1.6	.6
2,000-5,000	2.3	6.0	4.4	1.4	.6
5,000-10,000	2.2	5.8	4.0	1.2	.5
10,000-25,000	2.7	5.6	3.8	1.2	.5
25,000-50,000	2.7	5.2	3.6	1.1	.3
50,000 and over	2.2	5.2	3.7	1.1	.5
Average	2.4	5.9	4.4	1.3	.5

Source: *Statistische Berichte*, 1965, 1967, 1969, 1971, 1972. The "average" vote figures in this table differ slightly from those elsewhere because absentee ballots are not included in these calculations.

marschen into a stronghold, but here the similarity
of regional concentration stops. In his comparison
of voting in the Weimar Republic and in the Federal
Republic, Heinz Sahner found only modest correlations between NSDAP and NPD electoral strength; the
correlations between the NSDAP and the CDU are
considerably higher (see Table IV-4). The decisive
differences between NSDAP and NPD strength lie in
the NPD's limited success in Geest areas but significant following in Oldenburg—quite the reverse of
the Nazi pattern. In fact the geographic distinction between marsh, Geest, and hill country, which
Heberle used to illustrate important political
differences, no longer is very illuminating; the
differences in the NPD vote in the three areas are
negligible. One has only to look at the electoral
maps to see that new regional concentrations have
replaced the old.[11]

Ecological analysis, in addition to showing
regional concentrations of NPD support, also yields
clues about the social origins of NPD voters. The
safest inference concerns one prominent group that
does not vote NPD, namely urban workers. Urban
working-class districts display comparatively low
levels of NPD voting (see Table IV-5). Sahner found
a small negative correlation between NPD voting and
industrial workers (-0.17), and no significant
correlation between NPD voting and farm laborers
(+0.03).[12] He also found no significant correlations between NPD voting and (1) officials (*Beamte*),

Table IV-4

*Correlations of NSDAP, NPD, and CDU
Voting Patterns*

| | NSDAP | | |
	1928	*1930*	*1932*
CDU 1967	.34	.58	.63
NPD 1967	.16	.31	.22

Source: Sahner, *Politische Tradition,
Sozialstruktur und Parteiensystem in Schleswig-Holstein,*
p. 111.

(2) employees (*Angestellte*), and (3) refugees.
Between NPD voting and farmers there exists a modest
positive correlation.[13]   All these calculations
suggest that the NPD recruits from all classes, with
proportionately more adherents coming from farmers
and proportionately fewer from the urban working
class.

From the very earliest studies of the NPD there
has been speculation that the refugee population
provides a disproportionately high share of NPD
votes.[14]   On the basis of this hypothesis Schleswig-
Holstein, with some 20 to 30 percent of its population consisting of refugees, ought to offer fertile
soil for right-wing radicalism. Electoral analysis
reveals, however, that there is no significant
correlation between the percentage of refugees and
the percentage of NPD voters. The data show that
the SPD vote increases slightly with the percentage
of refugees and that the CDU vote decreases somewhat, but there is no evidence to indicate that the
refugees in Schleswig-Holstein constitute a group
particularly responsive to the blandishments of the
NPD.[15]

Military officers are another social group
sometimes considered a reservoir of NPD supporters.
This claim is hard to investigate through ecological analysis because German officials are reluctant to disclose the location of military bases, but
the available evidence provides little support for
it. To cite only two examples: Plön, the site of
a sizable army garrison, did give the NPD 7.3
percent of the vote in 1967 and 4.6 percent in 1969,

Table IV-5

NPD Votes in Urban Working-Class Areas

	1965	1967	1969
Lübeck (districts 117-131)	1.9	5.2	3.3
Kiel Gaarden-Ost	1.3	4.1	2.7
Flensburg (district 8)	0.7	2.4	2.6
Schleswig-Holstein as whole (all areas, urban and rural)	2.4	5.8	4.3

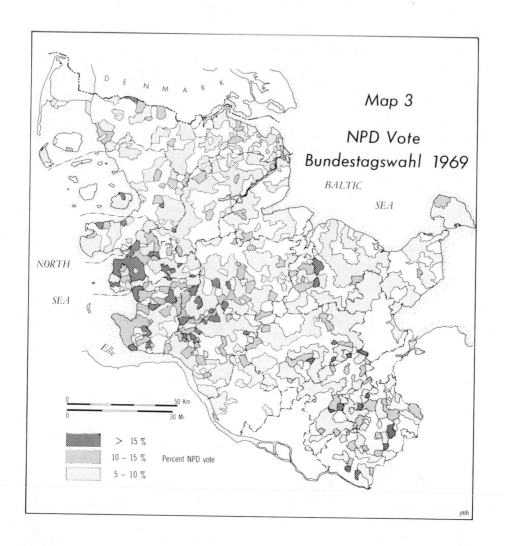

but Jagel, in *Kreis* Schleswig where an air base is
located, yielded only 3.5 percent in 1967 and 1.3
percent in 1969. The party chairman claims that
prior to the 1969 election numerous professional
soldiers had joined the party, but as they observed
that NPD members were not promoted, they left the
party.[16]

As one turns to an analysis of NPD members
rather than voters, a slightly different picture
appears. First, in the membership profile of the
NPD in Schleswig-Holstein, middle-class and farm
elements clearly dominate. Because obtaining
information about characteristics of NPD members is
difficult, the figures available may be subject to
error, but it is clear that party members come overwhelmingly from traditional middle-class occupations
with a modest sprinkling of recruits from the "new
middle class" and some army officers. Farmers
comprise over 50 percent of the membership.

Secondly, the presence of a high percentage of
NPD members is associated with a high percentage of
NPD voters. In mid-1969 the NPD counted just over
1,600 members; by *Kreis* the largest groups were
Steinburg 153, Kiel 148, Lübeck 123, Rendsburg 104,
and Eutin 102. Immediately one observes that the
largest *Kreis* groups do not produce the highest
percentages of NPD votes. If, however, one compares
those *Kreise* with the highest percentages of NPD
members with those with the highest percentages of
NPD voters, then the interrelationship between the
presence of party members and voters becomes
apparent. Table IV-6 lists the seven (overwhelmingly rural) *Kreise* with the highest percentage of
NPD members and illustrates the fact that these
Kreise have consistently had an NPD vote well above
the *Land* average. Regional concentrations of NPD
members, then, largely coincide with concentrations
of NPD voters. This coincidence might result simply
from the fact that certain sociological determinants
act more powerfully in these areas, but the data
also allow the conclusion that influential party
members may be responsible for local electoral
successes, a possibility which—as will become
apparent—is in fact the case.

The third type of evidence regarding NPD
supporters, public opinion polling data, is small in
amount and limited in utility. National surveys
poll too few Schleswig-Holsteiners for their data to
be reliable for analysis at the *Land* level, but the

Table IV-6

NPD Members and NPD Voting

Kreis	NPD members as percentage of voting population	NPD vote in: 1965	1967	1969
Steinburg	.18	2.9	6.5	4.9
Oldenburg	.17	3.9	8.2	5.2
Flensburg-Land	.16	2.8	5.8	5.0
Eiderstedt	.15	3.5	6.3	4.9
Eutin	.15	3.0	6.8	4.8
Süderdithmarschen	.14	2.7	7.4	6.7
Norderdithmarschen	.12	2.9	7.6	6.4
Average Schleswig-Holstein	.09	2.4	5.8	4.3

data that are available indicate once again that
while the NPD draws support from various social
strata, farmers are the class most susceptible to
its appeals. The earliest opinion surveys show that
the NPD was slow in attracting support among any
portion of the voting public (see Table IV-7). In
late 1968, however, *Die Welt* reported new poll
results which showed a considerable rise in NPD
sentiment among farmers in Niedersachsen and
Schleswig-Holstein: while in a comparable 1966
survey only 1.4 percent had expressed a preference
for the NPD, in 1968 11.4 percent did so. In the
same period the percentage of CDU supporters dropped
from 63.6 percent to 34.8 percent, with noncommittal
responses rising from 23 to 35 percent.[17] What
percentage of these NPD supporters were Schleswig-
Holsteiners and how many of them actually voted for
the NPD one has no way of knowing, but the poll
creates a further presumption in favor of the
thesis that while all classes provided NPD voters,
farmers contributed a disproportionately high
share.
        Which farmers were these? Were they the
marginal, debt-ridden farmers so often cited as the
major reservoir of Nazi votes in rural areas? A
number of analysts have so concluded:

        The year 1966, however, demonstrated that
        middle-sized farms that had previously been
        considered profitable and worth aspiring to
        were threatened: in Schleswig-Holstein
        imposing modern farms were sold at auction
        because the farmers could not pay back the
        loans they had used to rationalize their opera-
        tions; often they could not even pay the
        interest. From such forced auctions the
        Schleswig-Holstein farmers' route to the NSDAP
        took its starting point during the Weimar
        Republic. Since at the beginning of 1967 12
        percent of the farms in Schleswig-Holstein were
        hopelessly in debt and a further 25 percent
        acutely endangered, a similar development
        appears not to be out of the question.[18]

This explanation seems plausible and appealing, but
closer ecological analysis suggests that it is false.
        First, the NPD does better in areas where farm
incomes are relatively high; as noted above, the NPD
receives higher percentages of the vote in the more

Table IV-7

Profession of Head of Household and Attitude Toward NPD

| | Attitude toward NPD | | | | |
	Positive %	Indifferent %	Negative %	No Response %	Number of Respondents
Upper Middle Class (*Gehobener Mittelstand*)		17.2	69.0	13.8	29
Small Independent Proprietors (*Kleine Selbständige*)		30.0	50.0	20.0	30
Farmers (*Bauern*)	4.5	18.2	40.9	36.4	22
White Collar (*Kleine Angestellte u. Beamte*)	3.7	9.9	48.1	38.3	81
Workers (*Arbeiter*)	4.5	12.8	40.6	42.1	133
Housewives (*Hausfrauen*)	2.9	8.6	34.3	54.3	35

Source: Data Pool 1966, Zentralarchiv der Universität zu Köln. Period of Survey: March-November. Age of Respondents: 21–79. Cited in Sahner, *Politische Tradition, Sozialstruktur und Parteiensystem in Schleswig-Holstein*, p. 134.

prosperous farming areas of Dithmarschen and East
Holstein, but does not do well in the poorest
farming regions. Regional breakdowns of farm
incomes are difficult to obtain, but the *Landwirtschaftskammer's* survey of bookkeeping farmers in
fiscal year 1967-68 discloses that the *Kreise* of
Oldenburg and East Holstein and the grain farmers of
the west coast had the highest incomes per hectare.
Compared to a Schleswig-Holstein average income of
213 Deutsche Marks (DM) per hectare, Oldenburg
farmers earned 463 DM per hectare, East Holstein
farmers 296 DM per hectare, and west coast grain
growers 333 DM per hectare. These areas also
contain the largest farms, strongly implying that the
farmers here will have substantially higher returns
on their total acreage than farmers elsewhere. Yet
all of these areas had levels of NPD voting substantially above the average for rural areas. Thus, the
hypothesis that farmers operating on the margin of
profitability constitute the basis of NDP support
does not appear tenable; if this explanation were
true, then the Geest with its below average farm
income (174 DM per hectare) ought to be the center
of NPD strength.[19]
     One might try to rescue the hypothesis by
stressing the possibility of highly indebted farmers
within prosperous areas, but this approach encounters two difficulties. First, not all indebtedness
is burdensome: one man's debt is another's venture
capital. The general level of indebtedness has
continued to climb, however, until 17 percent of all
farms carry over 3,200 DM per hectare of debt, a
level considered quite excessive.[20] But (and this
is the second difficulty) the available statistics
do not disclose precisely where these endangered
farms are located. Two bits of information, however,
hint strongly that the greatest number of marginal
farms lie on the Geest rather than in the coastal
areas where the NPD has its bastions. First, the
smaller the farm, the higher the load of borrowed
capital and interest (see Table IV-8) — and the
smallest farms are on the Geest; both Dithmarschen
and East Holstein have farms of above average size.
Secondly, a regional breakdown discloses that in
mid-1968 the load of debt (with the important exclusion of farms over 100 hectares) was highest on the
east coast; east coast farmers carried an average of
1,786 DM per hectare, Geest farmers 1,691, and west
coast farmers 1,544.[21] These figures do not correlate well with regional variations in the NPD vote,

Table IV-8

Debt and Interest Loads 1968

Size of Farm in Hectares	Borrowed Capital DM/hectare	Interest Rates %	Interest in DM/hectare
10-20	2,154	4.97	107
20-50	2,057	4.86	100
50-100	1,757	4.67	82
Over 100	1,650	4.24	70

Source: Landwirtschaftskammer Schleswig-Holstein, *Die Produktionsstruktur in der schleswig-holsteinischen Landwirtschaft*, p. 21.

although they do suggest that indebtedness may be a better explanation of NPD voting in rural areas of East Holstein than it is in Dithmarschen. Dithmarschen itself sharply contradicts the view of the NPD voter as a debt-ridden marginal farmer; there one finds high levels of income and comparatively low burdens of debt combined with high NPD voting. In short, contrary to Kühnl's thesis and to the Weimar experience, the economically endangered small farmer no longer forms the basis of radical rightist politics.

Instead the NPD voters in the marshes are often what I shall call *marginal upper-class farmers*, the lordly marsh farmers who formerly relied exclusively upon hired labor and who are now forced to do the work on the farm themselves, the former conspicuous consumers now obliged to live comfortably rather than expansively. Their farms used to provide generous surpluses for easy upper-class living; now they produce just another middle-class income. Their 40 to 75 hectare farms exceed the average farm in size and profitability; their operations are far from being marginal in the strict economic sense of the word, but they no longer allow the same high standard of living. Their owners have no intention of leaving agriculture; it is precisely because they intend to continue farming that they are so upset by recent developments.

The marginal upper-class farmers felt most keenly the unpleasant facts encapsulated in the

report that in 1966-67 the index of farm consumer
prices overtook the index of farm product prices
and that from the 1961-1963 period to 1968 the
prices of farm products rose only 2.9 percent.[22]
They were inclined to blame their declining fortunes
upon the effects of entrance into the European
Economic Community, upon the Community's agricultural policies as conducted by the Dutchman
Mansholt, and upon the German government's willingness to make concessions at their expense. They
refused to recognize the argument that no more
resources were available for agricultural subsidies.
Under these conditions men with a traditional inclination to national causes turned to the NPD, some
out of a firm conviction that Germany must pursue
more forcefully its national interests (by which
they meant agriculture), others from a desire to
extract further subsidies from a suitably frightened
CDU. The statistical evidence only hints of this
phenomenon, but local interviews (the fourth kind of
evidence concerning NPD voters) confirmed that
marginal upper-class farmers constitute a crucial
source of NPD support.[23]

These interviews also disclose that although
the marginal upper-class farmer is not the only NPD
voter in Dithmarschen and other rural regions, his
presence is the decisive factor behind NPD successes. Through his power and reputation in the
community and in his circle of friends he draws
other voters to the NPD. He need not try to coerce
his neighbors; if they want to use his tractor or
gather some wood from his estate, they will be
careful not to alienate him. Nor does his influence
derive strictly from material incentives; the large
farmers are often the most active in community organizations—they have the most time for such activities—and through their efforts they earn respect
and friendship. When such a man joins the NPD (or
the CDU or the FDP), he brings others with him; he
is an opinion-maker.

In Dithmarschen the NPD *Landtag* representative,
Wolfgang Ehlers, is such a man. A member of the
hunting club and riding school, a school board
member for a vocational school in Büsum, active in
the local veterans' organization, Ehlers is an
important local figure. When he speaks for the NPD,
his associates and their families grant him a
hearing. In his neighborhood the NPD fares well;
its support begins to fade the closer one approaches

the home of the CDU *Bundestag* representative,
Hermann Glüsing.[24]

How important these local personalities are in
generating the NPD vote can be seen in another NPD
stronghold, the farm villages west of Preetz in
Kreis Plön. In Pohnsdorf the NPD received 14.1
percent of the vote in 1967 (27 votes) and managed
to increase its percentage to 16.9 percent in 1969
(33 votes). It is no mere coincidence that the
local party spokesman, Peter Jäger, lives in Pohnsdorf. Together with his brother, Jäger operates an
efficient modern farm of 75 hectares, an estate
which Jägers have farmed since 1500. Jäger begins
his political speeches with a description of the
farm and his agricultural operations, cites his
record of success (which, he claims, his audiences
already know), and then he turns to questions of
agricultural policy, arguing for higher prices and a
strong national protectionist policy for German
farmers. Outside Pohnsdorf he convinces disgruntled
farmers, but within the village personal animosities
have kept him from making converts of other farmers.
Instead the NPD voters in Pohnsdorf—Jäger's
friends—come from a variety of occupations; they
include a mechanic, a brick-layer, and a farm-
worker. Jäger's immediate family contributes seven
votes, roughly a quarter of the local total. In
such small communities a man of even modest reputation, his family, and his friends can suffice for an
impressive NPD showing. Where the man's prestige
begins to wane and other personalities dominate, NPD
strength dwindles; in the nearby Probstei, the area
north and west of Preetz, Jäger's propaganda has
failed to crack the CDU tradition of the leading
farmers.

Just why some isolated local notables have
become NPD spokesmen is not clear; a local spat or
feud which may have little to do with national politics has often provided the stimulus. Former adherents of the highly nationalist Schleswig-Holstein
CDU need not adapt much to feel at home in the NPD;
if the local CDU passes over them or offers little
opportunity for political advancement, some have
chosen to cast their lot with the NPD, a party which
promises instant leadership and which—at one time—
offered brighter prospects than the FDP. Young men
in particular have preferred rapid advancement in
the NPD to the long, slow struggle for prominence in

the CDU. Both Ehlers and Jäger were former CDU men
who became disillusioned, Jäger because of "bad
experiences" with the party in local politics.[25]
But fallings-out with the CDU may not provide the
whole explanation; both Ehlers and Jäger are men of
considerable education whose training (their
acquaintances feel) equips them for something
better. Both have met frustrations in their careers
which may have led them to seek political prominence
outside conventional channels. But one can only
speculate about these psychological motives.

The importance of local personalities helps
explain the peculiar scattering of the NPD vote and
helps to illuminate the broad class composition of
the party's electorate; but of course the presence
of local notables cannot explain the entire NPD
vote. The NPD receives votes where it has no
outstanding representatives; in such cases voters
are often marginal middle-class types. In the
village of Blekendorf in the eastern part of *Kreis*
Plön, a struggling innkeeper is a staunch but
discreetly quiet NPD partisan. A number of other
marginal members of this community, including one
who has served a prison sentence, support the NPD.
Around Schleswig the NPD serves as a home for
natural "'ginners," men who are against everything,
and for inefficient (as opposed to marginal)
farmers. Throughout the province one hears of
irreconcilable Nazis and their sons voting NPD, but
such instances are relatively infrequent, except on
the west coast.

NPD voters, then, as the evidence from voting
statistics, opinion surveys, and local interviews
indicates, are a heterogeneous group, recruited from
all sectors of the rural population but especially
from farmers. Progressive, prospering farmers tend
to retain their allegiance to the CDU, but farmers
large and small who are less capable find an explanation of their difficulties in NPD propaganda.
They vote for the party partly out of conviction,
but more as a protest and as a warning to the CDU.
The larger farmers among them, and especially the
marginal upper-class farmer in Dithmarschen, pull
recruits from family and friends, thus producing
regional concentrations of NPD support. Piqued by
mistreatment at the hands of the local CDU, these
men gravitate to the NPD, lured by the prospect of
instant authority, and form there a "bourgeois club"

of disgruntled nationalists sprinkled with just
enough brutes with a Nazi past to worry foreigners
and good German democrats.

So considerable was (and is) rural disillusion-
ment with CDU agricultural policy that the surprising fact is that the NPD succeeds no better than
it does. Within the *Bauernverband*, in public
forums, and at CDU assemblies the farmers recite the
litany of complaints against the agricultural policy
of the EEC and the government: unfair competitive
conditions, slick dealing by foreigners, inadequate
price policies, and a host of further grievances.
If the CDU wins a farmer's support, he specifies
that it is only because the party represents the
least of evils; the ranks of fervid rural CDU
supporters have thinned considerably in recent years.
Numerous farmers lament that the NPD's agricultural
policy is really more attractive, but that it simply
is not possible to vote for the party. Such behavior is—in most areas—just not respectable.

The "tyranny of the majority," which in specific local areas once effectively coerced the
reluctant into Nazi membership, now sharply limits
and constrains the activities of the NPD. There has
emerged a formidable public consensus against the
party. In case after case NPD activists report
social pressure, ostracism, and threatened loss of
livelihood. On the day preceeding the 1967 election
a female candidate left the party; pressure from her
husband's employer was given as the reason.[26] Party
leaders speak of pressure brought upon their
employers to release them, and they claim that members face the same sanctions. Unions refuse to
accept NPD members.[27] Large CDU farmers discourage
smaller, potential NPD adherents. The army denies
promotion to officers associated with the party.
The church condemns the party.

While in the late days of the Weimar Republic
the Nazis in Schleswig-Holstein benefited from
nearly unanimous support in the bourgeois press,
today even mildly favorable coverage for the NPD can
be found in only one paper—a small and uninfluen-
tial weekly based in Dithmarschen. Radio and tele-
vision give no favorable publicity to the NPD.
Small town merchants, who once would have had no
choice but to become Nazis or face a crippling
boycott, now must avoid any open gesture of support
for the NPD. The force of social pressure extends
to the families and relatives of NPD leaders. One
party candidate's son received notes from his

schoolmates: "NPD Nein, ADF [a minute Communist party] Ja"; another's niece was asked in school if her father was the NPD activist. The point is clear: anyone who chooses to engage in NPD politics is likely to face considerable harassment except perhaps in certain sections of Dithmarschen.

These social pressures originate from a variety of sources. In urban areas the unions and the SPD constitute the NPD's staunchest foes, but in the countryside Social Democratic influence wears thin. Here the CDU subtly poisons the well for the NPD. The elder generation does not argue doctrinal points nor debate programs, but pins the "neo-Nazi" label securely to the party and issues a series of grim warnings: "We've seen where that all leads once before"; "Don't hurt Germany's position in the world by voting for the NPD"; and finally, "If you don't vote CDU, you'll get SPD." The younger, more progressive contingent within the CDU, joined by young colleagues from other parties, takes the battle to the enemy; youthful hecklers and critics often outnumbered all other groups at NPD meetings. Between 1928 and 1933 Nazi speakers faced far more receptive audiences and reaped applause from young men whose contemporary counterparts picket and quarrel with NPD speakers. The effect of thoroughly disillusioned Nazis turned democrats is incalculable, but certainly not to be underestimated. The churches quietly contribute. And above all, the media hammer home the message that the NPD is a dangerous party domestically and an awkward embarrassment internationally.

To be effective any propaganda effort must find responsive chords in its hearers. Were the people of Schleswig-Holstein not generally disposed against a repetition of the Nazi experience, worried about the possible reaction of West Germany's allies, and disinclined to any kind of political turmoil, then the campaign of the press, parties, and other groups would have little effect. But Schleswig-Holsteiners recall the flood of refugees from the advancing Soviet armies, the costs of defeat, and the revelations of the atrocities against the Jews; they have "seen where all that can lead."[28] Nazism—or more precisely, defeat—serves as an effective antidote to any desire to repeat history, even as farce.

Women in particular identify the NPD as a threat to peace and security and refuse to support it. Many people recognize the nation's strategic and economic dependence upon its Western allies and

wish at all costs to avoid falling within the orbit
of the Soviet Union. And rural people will concede
in candid moments that the CDU's sprinkling can has
showered a profusion of benefits and subsidies upon
them—and that in the future the CDU will be far
more receptive to their pleas than the SPD. For in
a country gravitating toward a two-party system, the
threat of a wasted vote becomes real. In a close
election a vote withheld from the CDU puts the SPD
that much closer to power; it is one thing to cast
a vote for a radical party in a multi-party system
in which governments emerge from mysterious negotia-
tions among obscure politicians, quite another to
vote for radical reaction when it could put "the
reds" in power.

     Against these obstacles the mediocre leadership
of the NPD has made little headway; they have no
program beyond a suspect nationalism and a reactionary *Mittelstandspolitik*. Their platform is
tailored to the possibilities of another era, the
late Weimar Republic, not to the Germany of the late
1960s. The middle-class elements which would
respond to their promises have contracted sharply
and the petty bourgeois stratum which remains has,
despite its complaints, never had it so good. Farm
spokesmen privately admit that farmers' present
difficulties bear no relation to those of the late
twenties. Farm incomes have shown a rising secular
trend, although rural incomes have lagged behind
urban ones. In fiscal year 1967-68 farmers with 20
to 50 hectares had gross incomes of 7-12,000 DM.[29]
New buildings, the best indicator of farm prosperity, have sprung up. Farmers have built up their
livestock herds substantially.[30] All this evidence
of economic modernization and improvement amply
indicates that by any objective assessment the
current economic situation is far better than that
in 1928-33. The level of economic dissatisfaction
is correspondingly lower; neither sociological nor
economic conditions offer the NPD the same opportunities as the Nazis. Consequently, the NPD's
strategy for recruitment can only be termed an
anachronism.

     In summary, the NPD in rural Schleswig-Holstein
has recruited members across class lines, but it
relies to a large extent upon the influence of the
marginal upper-class farmer. In Dithmarschen, in
Kreis Plön west of Preetz, in Oldenburg, and in
other scattered areas these personalities have

succeeded in establishing concentrations of NPD
voters. Throughout the *Land* the party has also
drawn upon a small reservoir of dedicated supporters
of nationalist and reactionary causes. The party's
brief flourishing in 1967 can be traced to a declining agricultural prosperity unanticipated by the
CDU. Given, however, the social pressures against
NPD affiliation, the massive anti-NPD campaign, the
reluctance to relive the Nazi experience, the inept-
ness of the NPD leadership, the general economic
prosperity, and some further factors to be discussed
in the next chapter, the NPD episode was destined to
be short-lived.

5: Nazi Success and NPD Failure in Rural Schleswig-Holstein: Conclusions

Reinhard Kühnl and his colleagues in their book, *Die NPD, Struktur, Ideologie und Funktion einer neofaschistischen Partei*,[1] argue that the Federal Republic bears perilous structural resemblances to Weimar and that if the NPD is allowed free rein, history may repeat itself as catastrophe.

> Our thesis holds that what separates the second German democracy from the first are—with a few exceptions which will be noted—superficial appearances: the basic structures have changed only slightly.[2]

The authors view the NPD as a clearly Fascistic party and strongly imply that a serious economic depression would result in a resurgence, if not a recurrence, of Fascism. They make no effort to hide their understandable dissatisfaction with the existing social and political structure of the Federal Republic, but this dissatisfaction often blinds them to real historical differences. In what follows I shall compare the electoral support of the NSDAP and of the NPD, try to account for the differences in their appeal, and finally consider some theoretical implications.

Geographically the NSDAP began in the cities, propagandized intensively to build up strongholds on the west coast (relying on the personal efforts of dedicated antirepublicans, like the members of the Ehrhardt brigade who settled in Lockstedter Lager), gradually spread east and north, and eventually

received its most concentrated support on the
Schleswig Geest. It did least well in East Holstein
and the area around Hamburg. Socially the party
recruited very successfully among middle-class
farmers and the rural petty bourgeoisie—shopkeepers, craftsmen, and the like. Some larger farmers,
especially in Dithmarschen, lent their influence to
the National Socialist cause, but elsewhere wealthier
farmers were inclined to view the National Socialists
as *nicht standesgemäss*, not quite proper fellows to
associate with. Rural laborers, where they could
afford the luxury of an independent political
opinion (viz., in East Holstein where they were well
unionized), rejected Nazism, but in the cohesive
communities on the Geest and to a lesser extent in
the marshes, they supported the party of their
employers—to what extent from fear or from conviction one cannot say. Politically the NSDAP absorbed
above all disaffected "liberal" voters, dissolving
their tenuous attachment to the loosely organized
bourgeois parties.

The necessary conditions for the Nazis' electoral success (only!—the following list does not
purport to explain the Nazi seizure of power) can be
classified under five headings. The first may be
termed demographic. The Nazis' strongest support
came from rural areas, and the heaviest concentrations of their 63.8 percent of the rural vote
occurred where middle-class farmers, shopkeepers,
and craftsmen predominated. The small or medium
farmer, celebrated in America as the sturdy prop of
Jeffersonian democracy, proved most receptive to
Nazi appeals. It is an obvious but important point
that this group and those dependent upon them still
constituted a numerous and significant class at the
end of the Weimar Republic. The censuses of 1925
and 1933 revealed that 30 percent of the working
population engaged in agriculture; of these about
a fifth were independent property holders, over two-
fifths family help, and the remainder (about a
third) hired employees.[3] The percentage of people
employed in the secondary sector of the economy had
overtaken the percentage of those engaged in agriculture, but one could still speak of Schleswig-
Holstein as an *Agrarland* without serious inaccuracy.
In short, the potential rural reservoir of Nazi
voters remained quite large.

A second necessary condition of Nazi success
may be termed ideological. The NSDAP skillfully

exploited nationalist and reactionary currents in
the rural people's traditional view of the political
world, and thus succeeded in turning economic hard-
ships into a political crisis. The strongly nationalist sentiments, the irritation at the loss of
North Schleswig, the hatred for Marxism and socialism, the traditional antipathy to centralized
control (and at the same time the confident expectation of state aid in time of troubles), the longing
for clean government, and stringent adherence to
received moral tenets—all of these feelings the
Nazis tapped and employed for their own ends,
building upon the foundation provided by earlier
rightist movements and nationalist organizations.
The character and strength of these traditions
facilitated NSDAP penetration and largely explain
the negligible opposition to the party from bourgeois sources.

A third essential condition of Nazi success was
economic distress. The combination of a structural
crisis engendered by the pampering of German agriculture behind high tariff barriers and a cyclical
crisis originating in market imbalance, bad weather,
and decreased urban consumption wrought real hardship upon Schleswig-Holstein farmers. Some of them
had turned to Nazism before the depression, and
others never accepted the party even with the
depression, but many responded to the Nazi call for
release from the burden of debt and interest payments (*"Entschuldung und Brechung der Zinsknecht-
schaft"*). Firm in their conviction that the government owed them assistance, the farmers at first
placed their faith in the bourgeois parties and the
farm lobbying organizations; when these groups
failed to extract aid in sufficient quantity, the
farmers paid heed to appeals for more radical
remedies.

The failure to obtain governmental assistance
leads to a fourth condition for Nazi success, the
structure of the political system. The ways in
which the organization of the regime obstructed the
possibilities for genuine relief of farmers is a
topic in itself, as Alexander Gerschenkron's mas-
terly *Bread and Democracy in Germany* indicates.
Gerschenkron shows in detail how the Social Democrats were limited in aiding farmers by their obli-
gations to their urban voters. Higher farm prices
entailed higher food prices for urban workers, whose
budgets were already tight; higher taxes to provide

subsidies would have had a similarly constricting
effect upon their consumption. Furthermore, the
Social Democrats were slow to recognize that large
portions of the Schleswig-Holstein farmers differed
from the Junkers—that the difficulties of the
former were real. Nor should one neglect the effect
of the depression upon governmental revenues; even
conservative governments could not grant adequate
aid without the resources to do so. The Nazis
exploited this situation by arguing that farmers, as
a minority in an industrial democracy, could never
receive just treatment of their claims; only as the
first class of the Third Reich might they find
satisfaction.[4]

The party system also contributed greatly to
Nazi success in two major ways. First, the lack of
organization among the bourgeois parties offered the
Nazi organizers little resistance. The liberal
parties and to a lesser extent the DNVP had remained
Honoratiorenparteien, loose coalitions assembled
around local notables. The liberal parties failed
to organize leaders or followers in rural areas;
consequently when their program and performance no
longer appealed, there were no organizational loyalties, no local offices, no party services to brake
the flow of voters away from their ranks. To say
that their organization dissolved would be incor-
rect; it never existed. Secondly, the variety of
bourgeois parties meant that electoral results need
not determine the shape and texture of the government coalition; politicians in Berlin, not voters in
Schleswig-Holstein, created governments. One might
as well vote for an obscure new party as for the
older cliques:

> ...the nonsocialist camp lacked a crystalliza-
> tion point that could draw the former voters of
> the DVP, DDP, and above all of the DNVP to it.
> Here lay...in the time of upheaval and disorder
> the greatest chance for the NSDAP, still weak
> and unestablished in the province.[5]

The bourgeois parties could not fall back on the
traditional loyalties and organizational services
that sustained the SPD, and thus when crisis came,
the most energetic and well-organized party stood
the greatest chance of success.

The energy and organization of the NSDAP constitutes the fifth essential condition of Nazi

success.   No one can gainsay the remarkable organizational feats of this party.   Where previous
radical reactionary movements had floundered for
lack of funds (despite sizable contributions), the
Nazis pressed ahead, substituting manpower for money
when necessary.   Nazi campaigns could be called
well-orchestrated, but the metaphor is misleading
because it is not a military one.   The National
Socialists militarized politics; an electoral
campaign was a military operation.   The campaign
meetings were planned like so many battles; the
logistics of moving troops (SA and SS) were carefully worked out.   The entire army was mobilized for
a total effort.[6]   The strategy brought new conquests
and heightened the morale of previous recruits; as
Heberle says,

> The peculiar mass appeal of this party probably
> was due to a large extent to the fact that the
> Nazis created not merely another party but an
> entirely new type of political machine which
> constituted a totalitarian movement in a double
> sense: first, in that it aimed at a monopoly
> of political power; second, in that it was not
> merely a fee-collecting organization but
> claimed the entire man, demanding an exceed-
> ingly intensive participation in party work by
> its members.   In this fashion, the movement
> offered a psychic outlet for the repressed
> ambitions and emotions of rural youth; it lent
> prestige and authority to persons of mediocre
> or subordinate positions in ordinary ways of
> life.[7]

Energy, organization, invincibility—these were the
characteristics the party sought to embody and to
impart.   And it did.   To the undecided the NSDAP
appeared as a source of raw energy powerful enough
to alter political and economic conditions; this
impression helped overcome scruples about Nazi
brutality.   To others the NSDAP appeared as an
irresistible object, to which resignation was the
only prudent policy: "'It no longer makes sense to
try to do anything,' people said.   'We can do
nothing against the Nazi specter, but must endure
it.'"[8]
     Beside the NSDAP the NPD of Schleswig-Holstein
looks tame.   Its leaders lack the vigor and ruthless
energy of the Nazi commanders—poor leadership is a

common explanation of the NPD's lack of success. To
some extent the fear of legal sanctions imposes
restraints upon the party (a fear foreign to Nazi
leaders, for the good reason that they had little to
fear from the right judges), but more importantly
the NPD leaders are simply a different breed of men,
frustrated perhaps, but fundamentally comfortable,
secure, and dull. Their lackluster performance is
one major reason why their party has failed to
attract more voters.

The reasons for the NPD's failure tend to be
the obverse of the explanations for the NSDAP's
success. The party's inadequate leadership and
organization have already been noted. Demographic
factors further account for NPD difficulties. The
party has aimed its most intensive propaganda at a
declining class; with the modernization of the
economy the petty bourgeoisie that flocked to the
Nazis has shrunk considerably in size and importance. The percentage of the working population
engaged in agriculture now hovers around 11 or 12
percent, compared to 30 percent at the time of the
Nazi seizure of power. A larger percentage of these
people are independent entrepreneurs—the trend to
the family farm is clear—but the weight of this
group within the population has been declining since
1933 and is continuing to decline.[9] This decline
results from the emigration of rural people from the
agricultural sector of the economy to urban employment.

A second demographic fact may shed light on
barriers to NPD success. A 1949 survey showed
remarkable differences in fertility among small and
large farmers (see Table V-1). If one can equate
limited acreage with economic marginality, a sound
assumption in many cases, then it follows that
marginal farmers are having fewer children, and thus
the pool of people in perilous economic circumstances is expanding less rapidly (other things
being equal) than the pool of those in more favorable circumstances. Unfortunately there do not seem
to be comparable statistics for the 1920s, but
contemporary reports suggest larger families on
marginal farms than at present. A tempting, but
tentative, conclusion suggests itself: a higher
percentage of the rural population in the 1920s
lived in marginal economic circumstances—even in
prosperous periods and according to the standards
of marginality of that era.

Table V-1

*Relations between Size of Farm and Number
of Children in Schleswig-Holstein, 1949*

Farm Size in Hectares (Arable land only)	Children under Age 14 as % of	
	Family members living in home of farm operator	Farm proprietors
0 ha.	8.7	15
1-2 ha.	22.6	77
2-5 ha.	23.3	87
5-10 ha.	23.0	94
10-20 ha.	24.3	109
20-50 ha.	24.9	115
50-100 ha.	25.9	123
Over 100 ha.	29.5	140
All Sizes	23.8	99

Source: Gunther Thiede, *Regionale Unterschiede in der Arbeitsverfassung der
Schleswig-Holsteinischen Landwirtschaft* (Kiel, 1953), p. 26.

Today's rural Schleswig-Holsteiner does not
carry about the same ideological cargo as his counterpart in the 1920s and early 1930s. Much of the
old baggage is still there, it is true, but usually
in a modified form. The distrust of socialism still
persists, intensified among the elder generation by
bitter experience with the Soviet Union, alleviated
among younger rural people who recognize the *embour-
geoisement* of the SPD and begin to recognize it as
an electoral possibility. The strong nationalism
persists, carefully tended by the CDU, but the
change in Germany's international position has been
perceived and notions of the politically possible
appropriately lowered. The firm expectation of
state aid remains unabated—perhaps even increased
by habituation to CDU favors before and after elections. But changes are apparent. References to
Blut und Boden and similarly mystical and corpora-
tistic rhetoric evoke little response; pragmatism

is the order of the day. And most important, the
rural Schleswig-Holsteiner has seen "where that sort
of thing leads" and his children have been educated
to the same perspective. Thyge Thyssen may argue
that the agricultural community looks back upon the
Hitler years "without ill-will,"[10] but this observation holds only for the eldest and excludes the last
years of the regime. "Once was enough"—this dispo-
sition poses an enormous obstacle to the present
generation of right extremists.

     At least equally important in frustrating the
ambition of the nationalist right is the immense
alteration in economic conditions. Present-day
farmers, particularly the less progressive ones, may
encounter economic difficulties, but their problems
are moderate compared to those of farmers in the
late 1920s. Most important the contemporary farmer
can usually escape downward pressure on his income
in at least two ways: he can modernize his enterprise, or he can leave agriculture for urban employment. The possibility of the individual's liberat-
ing himself or his children from the plight of
employment in a declining industry is real; indeed
the government offers substantial incentives to
those who wish to leave agriculture. In the Weimar
period such a solution did not offer itself; the
crisis in the industrial economy eliminated the
chance of emigration to another sector of the
economy. Those farmers struck by the rural depression had no opportunity to flee to the cities; only
collective action could better their lot.

     The Weimar farmer was trapped on his marginal
farm; the present-day farmer is not. The importance
of this fact cannot be overestimated.[11] In the
1920s the differential between urban and rural
incomes was minimal; the romantic attractions of the
countryside celebrated by conservative ideologists
could be enjoyed at no loss in income. Today the
farmer's earnings lag well behind urban incomes and
instead of *Blut und Boden* one speaks of modernization and structural change (*Strukturwandel*)—of a
necessary accommodation to historical developments.
The rural Schleswig-Holsteiner is increasingly aware
of structural developments within the economy; he
appreciates the thickness of urban pay envelopes and
the availability of government inducements. He can
move out of the primary sector relatively comfortably; in numerous cases he need not move physically
but may simply commute. The decline of the agricul-

tural economy proceeds; the marginal farmer exits;
the "marginal upper-class farmer" remains as part of
a dwindling minority and pays the costs of delayed
modernization.

Should the marginal upper-class farmer consider
expressing his discontent by voting for the NPD,
some pertinent political considerations may dissuade
him. First, there arises the possibility that a
vote for the NPD rather than for the CDU may put the
SPD in office. Particularly when the CDU is in
opposition at the national level, the attraction of
voting NPD declines. Second, there is the likelihood that he may waste his vote; if the NPD fails to
amass 5 percent of the vote, his vote is in vain.
Third, there is the remembrance of past favors from
the CDU and the conviction that in all likelihood
no one else can offer more. Fourth, there is the
possibility of the loss of future influence upon the
local and regional CDU organization by open devia-
tion. Increasingly the CDU has penetrated local
politics and displaced the old loose bourgeois electoral alliances; to shape the course of events in
rural areas it becomes more and more necessary to
work from within the CDU.

From this comparative analysis there follow a
number of still more general conclusions of theoretical and practical interest. The most important
is that societies are susceptible to rural-based
movements of the extreme right only at certain
periods in their historical development. German
experience suggests that the greatest danger arises
when there are simultaneous rural and urban economic
crises. The rural crisis must be a structural one
stemming from delayed accommodation to modern agricultural practices and the consequent persistence of
marginal farming units and rural overpopulation; the
urban crisis must be sufficiently severe to prevent
a solution to the rural crisis through emigration to
the cities. Under these circumstances a sudden
cyclical depression in agriculture, accentuating the
structural crisis, produces the material for Fascism, particularly if the population has been trained
to think in the language of conservative nationalism. The prospects for Fascism decline sharply,
however, if the transition to modern agricultural
practices proceeds at a pace consistent with that of
international competitors, as it did in Denmark, or
if it proceeds concurrently with subsidized rural
emigration, as it now does in West Germany. In the
long run, modernization and emigration cause a

decline in the rural population that dries up the
reservoir of traditional Fascist support, forcing
movements of the extreme right to alter their
strategies or resign themselves to insignificance.

Given that the chances for rural-based Fascist
movements vary with the stage of rural development,
the study of such movements must also take into
account the effect of changing historical circumstances. Ahistorical forms of analysis which
concentrate their attention solely upon the status
anxieties of the middle class while failing to
observe the transformation in the composition of
this class must necessarily go astray. This failure
is precisely the flaw in the analysis of Kühnl and
his colleagues. Kühnl and others like him who have
emphasized the instability of the middle class and
the extent of the NPD danger may have contributed to
the public's disavowal of the party, but they have
distorted the scope of the original threat. Alarmed
by the prospect of a recurrence of Nazism, they have
missed crucial developments working against such an
outcome: the decline of the petty bourgeoisie,
changes in public consciousness, changes in the
structure of economic opportunities, and alterations
in the political system. Their concentration upon a
false target, a new NSDAP, has led to analytical
errors and to exaggeration of the NPD threat. However politically astute and commendable this technique may have been, it produced poor social
science.[12]

In an amusing irony, the NPD leadership has
committed the same analytical errors as its leftist
opponents. It continues to believe that it can
recruit from the same social strata that the Nazis
did, using a bowdlerized version of their appeals,
failing to realize that such an attempt is hope-
lessly anachronistic. The most consoling finding
about the NPD is that, like the SPD of the late
1920s and early 1950s, its leaders are unable to
adapt themselves to changing demographic, economic,
and political circumstances. As a practical conclusion, then, it follows that with its present strategy the NPD will not be a threat to political
stability. The prospects of a modernized neo-Nazi
party, operating in a period of economic depression
and exploiting the remaining pollution in the political atmosphere to develop an urban base, cannot be
accurately assessed, but the era of rural-based
Fascism has come to an end in West Germany.

Appendix I

Votes According to Size of Community 1949-1972

CDU

Population	1949	1953	1957	1961	1965	1969	1972
Under 1,000	30.6	50.9	54.4	50.6	58.0	62.9	52.3
1,000-2,000	32.9	46.5	47.9	44.5	51.7	57.0	46.4
2,000-5,000	31.8	46.6	44.8	39.5	47.1	52.4	42.7
5,000-10,000	30.9	45.0	45.2	39.6	48.7	54.2	44.1
10,000-25,000	29.9	44.9	44.9	38.7	46.1	50.9	41.5
25,000-50,000	22.2	40.9	42.5	39.0	45.5	48.3	39.2
Over 50,000	31.9	48.3	47.5	38.0	42.4	44.5	35.8

SPD

Population	1949	1953	1957	1961	1965	1969	1972
Under 1,000	27.1	20.2	22.7	27.8	28.9	30.6	40.5
1,000-2,000	30.1	25.1	28.8	33.6	35.1	36.1	45.7
2,000-5,000	30.3	26.0	31.6	36.4	39.3	40.6	48.5
5,000-10,000	30.8	27.8	32.9	38.3	38.1	38.8	46.6
10,000-25,000	31.4	28.9	34.0	39.4	40.3	42.6	49.0
25,000-50,000	24.7	26.8	33.0	37.0	40.6	44.1	50.0
Over 50,000	30.5	29.4	35.4	42.2	46.2	47.8	54.8

FDP

Population	1949	1953	1957	1961	1965	1969	1972
Under 1,000	5.8	3.7	4.3	13.8	10.2	2.9	6.3
1,000-2,000	7.8	4.6	4.7	13.4	10.2	3.4	7.2
2,000-5,000	7.3	4.2	5.8	14.2	10.1	4.0	8.1
5,000-10,000	9.8	5.7	6.6	14.7	9.8	4.0	8.4
10,000-25,000	8.1	5.5	6.6	14.3	9.5	4.0	8.8
25,000-50,000	10.3	7.0	7.2	15.5	9.7	4.6	10.0
Over 50,000	7.0	3.8	5.1	12.1	7.7	3.8	8.7

DP

Population	1949	1953	1957	1961 [GDP = DP + BHE]
Under 1,000	10.9	5.0	6.1	4.1
1,000-2,000	11.9	4.5	5.0	5.3
2,000-5,000	13.0	4.4	4.0	5.6
5,000-10,000	14.2	4.4	3.4	4.7
10,000-25,000	15.1	3.8	3.4	4.1
25,000-50,000	14.6	6.1	5.2	3.6
Over 50,000	9.4	2.5	1.8	2.3

SSW

(only in the seven northernmost "counties")

Population	1947	1948	1949	1953	1954	1957
Under 1,000		17.2	14.1	8.3	9.2	6.5
1,000-2,000		17.1	13.6	8.7	8.8	6.3
2,000-5,000		18.0	14.7	10.5	11.3	11.3
5,000-10,000		27.9	22.1	13.9	13.7	10.8
10,000-25,000		29.7	20.4	12.2	13.3	8.3
25,000-50,000		36.5	27.9	17.9	17.8	14.0
Over 50,000	60.7	49.0	44.0	32.2	36.1	26.2

GB/BHE

Population	1953	1957	1961
Under 1,000	15.4	9.3	4.1
1,000-2,000	14.9	11.1	5.3
2,000-5,000	13.4	10.5	5.6
5,000-10,000	12.7	10.3	4.7
10,000-25,000	11.5	8.9	4.1
25,000-50,000	10.9	8.1	3.6
Over 50,000	7.2	5.5	2.3

Extreme Right

Population	DKP 1949	DRP 1953	BdD+DRP 1957	DG+DRP 1961	NPD 1965	NPD 1969	NPD 1972
Under 1,000	2.1	0.8	0.9	1.0	2.2	2.0	.7
1,000-2,000	1.9	0.7	0.7	1.0	2.2	1.6	.6
2,000-5,000	1.5	1.0	0.9	0.9	2.3	1.4	.6
5,000-10,000	1.6	1.0	0.8	0.8	2.2	1.2	.5
10,000-25,000	1.7	1.2	1.0	0.9	2.7	1.2	.5
25,000-50,000	5.7	0.9	0.9	1.0	2.7	1.1	.5
Over 50,000	1.2	1.0	1.0	1.1	2.2	1.1	.4
Total	1.9	0.9	0.9	1.0	2.4	1.3	.5

Appendix II

Parties' Percentages of the Vote in Communities of Under 2,000 Inhabitants in the Three Natural Regions 1947-1965

	CDU	SPD	FDP	SSW	KPD	DKP	DP	GDP	BHE	NPD	Other Parties
Marsh											
1947	33.1	41.9	6.9	13.1	3.1	1.8	–	–	–	–	0.0
1962	48.0	30.6	13.7	4.0	–	–	–	3.1	–	–	0.7
1967	49.2	31.8	8.0	3.6	–	–	–	–	–	7.2	0.5
1953	44.9	22.9	5.8	4.8	0.6	–	7.9	–	12.1	–	1.0
1965	54.5	30.7	11.4	–	–	–	–	–	–	2.7	0.7
Geest											
1947	37.9	43.7	5.0	8.0	2.7	2.5	–	–	–	–	0.0
1962	55.4	26.4	11.6	1.6	–	–	–	4.1	–	–	0.9
1967	56.5	27.8	6.8	1.4	–	–	–	–	–	7.1	0.9
1953	50.5	19.3	4.5	2.3	0.7	–	5.9	–	15.7	–	1.1
1965	60.3	26.4	10.6	–	–	–	–	–	–	2.0	0.7
Hill Area											
1947	39.5	45.2	2.4	7.7	3.1	2.2	–	–	–	–	0.0
1962	48.3	34.5	9.1	1.8	–	–	–	5.6	–	–	0.8
1967	48.4	36.3	5.7	1.8	–	–	–	–	–	7.2	0.6
1953	49.8	23.6	3.0	2.7	0.7	–	2.6	–	16.2	–	1.2
1965	51.9	35.6	9.4	–	–	–	–	–	–	2.3	0.8

Source: Heinz Sahner, *Die NPD in der Landtagswahl 1967 in Schleswig-Holstein.* Diplomarbeit (Köln, 1969), p. 97.

Appendix III

Economic Structure and Party Vote in Major Subregions
(Communities under 2,000 inhabitants)

Party Vote and Percentages of Persons Employed
in Agriculture and Industry in Specific Marsh and Geest Regions

	Eider-stedt	Dithmarschen M	Dithmarschen G	Steinburg M	Steinburg G	Pinneberg M	Pinneberg G
Landtagswahl 1967							
CDU	39.16	45.81	56.23	47.55	52.37	55.43	52.94
SPD	28.66	36.78	30.36	36.68	30.48	33.75	35.36
FDP	17.35	6.34	5.65	8.05	8.37	5.56	5.06
NPD	6.50	10.83	7.51	7.22	8.23	4.83	5.52
Agriculture and Forestry							
Independent Proprietors	19.91	16.16	16.15	12.59	13.71	10.78	10.76
Family Help	24.10	20.91	25.42	17.57	19.80	15.68	15.05
Workers	5.91	15.09	6.01	7.17	8.91	9.20	9.51
Total*	49.92	52.16	47.58	36.33	42.42	35.66	35.32
Industry (Produzierende Gewerbe)							
Independent Proprietors	3.36	2.62	3.33	2.90	2.35	4.63	2.16
Family Help	0.76	0.68	0.96	0.79	0.67	0.82	0.49
Workers	16.91	22.42	24.37	31.19	30.35	35.55	35.88
Total	21.03	25.72	28.66	34.88	33.37	41.00	38.53

Appendix III (continued)

Party Vote and Percentages of Persons Employed
in Agriculture and Industry in Specific Hill Area Localities

	Flensburg	Schleswig (Angeln)	Eckernförde	Plön	Oldenburg
Landtagswahl 1967					
CDU	50.33	54.75	49.17	47.04	39.63
SPD	20.43	27.83	37.15	40.20	46.86
NPD	6.02	6.18	5.27	7.34	8.43
Agriculture and Forestry					
Independent Proprietors	12.82	13.83	12.13	11.90	9.90
Family Help	16.11	17.40	16.30	17.13	11.01
Workers	15.16	13.16	16.24	17.19	20.51
Total	44.09	44.39	44.67	46.22	41.42
Workers	46.94	47.18	52.90	54.92	59.66

Source: Sahner, *Politische Tradition, Sozialstruktur und Parteien-system in Schleswig-Holstein*, pp. 86, 91.

*The individual categories and the totals represent all those employed in this sector of the economy as a *percentage* of all the gainfully employed. Because there are other areas of employment (such as the civil service), the totals for the agricultural and forestry sector and the industrial sector, when combined, do not add up to 100 percent.

Notes

Introduction

1.   Barrington Moore, *Social Origins of Dicta-torship and Democracy* (Boston, 1966); Rudolf Heberle, *From Democracy to Nazism* (Baton Rouge, 1945).

2.   Moore, *Social Origins*, p. 477.

3.   Rudolf Heberle, *Landbevölkerung und Nationalsozialismus* (Stuttgart, 1963), p. 9.

4.   Heinz Sahner, *Die NPD in der Landtagswahl 1967 in Schleswig-Holstein*, Diplomarbeit. (Koln, 1969); Heinz Sahner, "Die NPD in der Landtagswahl vom 23.4.1967 in Schleswig-Holstein," in *Die NPD in der Landtagswahlen 1966-1968* (Köln, 1969); Heinz Sahner, *Politische Tradition, Sozialstruktur und Parteiensystem in Schleswig-Holstein* (*Politik und tradition*, Band 9) (Meisenheim am Glan, 1973).

5.   Communication to the author; John Nagle, *The National Democratic Party* (Berkeley, 1970), p. 140.

Chapter I: Ecology of Political Parties in Schleswig-Holstein, 1919-1933

1.   Professor Heberle conducted his research at the University of Kiel between 1932 and 1934 and observed the rise of National Socialism in Schleswig-Holstein at first hand. His work rests on an intensive ecological analysis of electoral statistics (here André Siegfried's *Tableau politique de la France de l'ouest sous la troisième république* [Paris, 1913] was clearly an inspiration) and on his own intimate knowledge of the various regions of Schleswig-Holstein and of the evolution of the farm interest groups. The coming of the Nazi dictator-ship removed any immediate opportunity for publish-ing the results of the research in full. A brief

article, "Die politische Haltung des Landvolks in
Schleswig-Holstein 1918-1932" (*Volksspiegel*, 1 Jg.
Nr. 4, 1934, pp. 166-172), appeared, but more extensive publication had to await Heberle's emigration
to the United States. First came two articles:
"The Political Movements among the Rural People in
Schleswig-Holstein, 1918-1932" (*Journal of Politics*,
1943, Vol. 5, No. 1, pp. 3-27 and Vol. 5, No. 2, pp.
115-142), and "The Ecology of Political Parties: A
Study of Elections in Rural Communities in
Schleswig-Holstein, 1918-1932" (*American Sociological Review*, Vol. XI, 1944, pp. 401-414). Then came
the first book-length treatment, in *From Democracy
to Nazism* (Baton Rouge, 1945; recently reissued New
York, 1970). Even this edition was incomplete and
superseded by the German publication of *Landbevölkerung und Nationalsozialismus: Eine soziologische
Untersuchung der politischen Willensbildung in
Schleswig-Holstein 1918 bis 1932* (Stuttgart, 1963).
Heberle has also discussed his methods and his
conclusions in *Social Movements* (New York, 1951) and
Hauptprobleme der politischen Soziologie (Stuttgart,
1967).

    2. Rudolf Heberle, *Landbevölkerung*, pp. 11-12.
This formulation is less cautious than the earlier
one in *From Democracy to Nazism*, p. 33: "The study
of rural political opinion encounters peculiar
obstacles since farmers and agricultural laborers,
and even great landlords, are not apt to express
their thoughts in speeches or writing. The rural
newspapers, never a very true expression of the
sentiments and opinions of farmers, represent them
less today than ever. The most immediate indicator,
and at the same time the only one which lends itself
to quantitative analysis, is the record of the
balloting in political elections."

    3. André Siegfried, *Tableau politique de la
France de l'ouest sous la troisième république*
(Paris, 1913), p. x.

    4. *From Democracy to Nazism*, pp. 23-31; *Land-
bevölkerung*, pp. 20-29. In a study strongly based
on Heberle's, Gerhard Stoltenberg, *Politische
Strömungen im schleswig-holsteinischen Landvolk
1918-1933* (Düsseldorf, 1962), the author also
stresses the contrast between the prewar period and
the end of the Weimar Republic. See especially
pp. 5, 7-8.

    5. *From Democracy to Nazism*, p. 32.

    6. Ibid., p. 31.

7. Ibid., p. 32.

8. Ibid., pp. 28-29.

9. "Whether the liberalism of these Progressives was anything more than a critique of protec-
tive tariff policies, only biographical studies
could show; it is thoroughly safe to say that the
farmers, and above all those west coast farmers who
leaned toward Progressivism, formulated their political opinions first of all with an eye to the interests of cattle raisers." Hans Beyer, "Landbevölkerung und Nationalsozialismus in Schleswig-
Holstein," *Zeitschrift für Agrargeschichte und
Agrarsoziologie*, Jg. 12, 1964, p. 71. Stoltenberg,
Politische Strömungen, p. 8, also makes this point.

10. See *Beiträge zur historischen Statistik
Schleswig-Holsteins* (hrsg. vom Statistischen
Landesamt Schleswig-Holstein, Kiel, 1967) p. 71.

11. Stoltenberg, *Politische Strömungen*, pp. 22-
23; Beyer, "Landbevölkerung," pp. 69-72.

12. Hermann Clausen, *Der Aufbau der Demokratie
in der Stadt Schleswig nach den zwei Weltkriegen:
Erinnerungen* (Flensburg, 1966), pp. 64ff., esp.
p. 71.

13. Heberle, *From Democracy to Nazism*, p. 91.

14. Although they have a different history,
these three regions are, as Heberle claims (e.g.
From Democracy to Nazism, p. 34), typical of other
regions of North Germany—the East Frisian marshes,
the Lüneburger Heide and the surrounding Geest
regions, and the eastern estate regions—and political developments in Schleswig-Holstein do shed
light on developments in the comparable regions; but
what makes Schleswig-Holstein most attractive for
study is not so much that it was typical, but that
it was an *extreme* case of Nazi success in a rural
area.

15. Heberle, "Ecology of Political Parties,"
p. 403; *From Democracy to Nazism*, p. 95.

16. In a speech at Rendsburg, 1 January 1921.
Cited by Heberle, *From Democracy to Nazism*, pp.
46-47.

17. See Stoltenberg, *Politische Strömungen*,
pp. 33-36, esp. p. 34.

18. Stoltenberg, *Politische Strömungen*, p. 33
footnote.

19. Heberle, *From Democracy to Nazism*, p. 46.
These comments on the party are largely indebted to
Heberle's own discussion, pp. 43-54. One should
note that the *Landespartei* did contain honorable

anti-Fascists. In private correspondence Professor
Heberle has pointed out to me that von Hedeman-
Heespen, an important figure in the party, seceded
when Lohse became too influential.

20. Heberle speaks of the DNVP's being "generally low on the Geest." "Ecology of Political
Parties," p. 405. *From Democracy to Nazism*, pp.
97-98. For the beginning and the end of the period
he is right, but in the 1924 elections the DNVP
achieved its higher percentages on the Geest. This
development suggests an early disenchantment with
the Weimar regime—*before* the onset of real economic
distress.

21. In the marsh areas of Dithmarschen, over
70 percent of the arable land rates on *Ackerzahl* of
66 or more. (The *Ackerzahl* gives information about
the agricultural suitability of land. Its basis is
the *Bodenzahl*, which measures the fertility of the
soil, supplemented by certain calculations which
assess the effect of the climate. The higher the
number, the better the conditions; a number over 65
is quite high.)

22. Heberle, *Landbevölkerung*, p. 52. The
German accounts, pp. 48-102, of society in the
various rural regions are much more detailed than
can be given here. They provide a superb picture of
rural life and deserve to be read not only as a
foundation to the theoretical sections, but also as
a qualification to the thrust of the theory.

23. Heberle, "Ecology of Political Parties,"
p. 407.

24. Heberle, *From Democracy to Nazism*, p. 36.

25. Cited in Stoltenberg, *Politische
Strömungen*, p. 31.

26. Heberle, *Landbevölkerung*, p. 55.

27. Ibid., and "Ecology of Political Parties,"
p. 408.

28. Heberle, *From Democracy to Nazism*, p. 103.

29. Heberle, *Landbevölkerung*, pp. 60-61.

30. See chapter two.

31. The following remarks are based largely on
Heberle, "Ecology," pp. 408-410; *Democracy to
Nazism*, pp. 104ff; and *Landbevölkerung*, p. 65ff.

32. Franz Osterroth, *Hundert Jahre Sozialdemokratie in Schleswig-Holstein* (Kiel, 1963).

33. Heberle, *Landbevölkerung*, pp. 72-73.

34. Ibid., p. 93. Once again this section
relies heavily on Heberle's unsurpassed descriptions, ibid. pp. 92-102. *From Democracy to Nazism*,

pp. 38ff. and pp. 108ff., and "Ecology," pp. 401-
411. See also Stoltenberg, *Politische Strömungen*,
p. 11, who also relies on Heberle.

35. Heberle, *From Democracy to Nazism*, pp.
38-39.

36. Heberle, *Landbevölkerung*, p. 100.

37. Heberle concludes his regional analysis by
"tentatively" stating that "while the decline of
liberalism and the growth of the counterrevolutionary parties were conditioned by the general
factor of economic distress, the subregional differ-
entials between the strength of the various parties
were primarily determined by the social structure of
the communities rather than directly by economic
factors." Heberle, "Ecology," p. 411. Strictly
speaking, the analysis demonstrates only the latter
point; it does not show that economic distress was
the general factor behind the rise of the counterrevolutionary parties—in fact I have not found any
place where Heberle presents evidence for the
contention that economic distress explains the turn
to the DNVP.

38. Heberle, "Ecology," p. 414.

39. Ibid.

40. See his pamphlet *Herunter mit der Maske* in
the archives at Schleswig, and Stoltenberg,
Politische Strömungen, pp. 151, 184.

41. "The methodology of electoral sociology is
in fact incomplete when it does not draw in to the
greatest possible extent investigations of the
sociology of political parties." Werner Conze,
"Wahlsoziologie und Parteigeschichte: Neue
französische Forschungen," *Aus Geschicte und Politik*
(Bergsträsser Festschrift), Düsseldorf, 1954, p.
250.

42. Heberle, "Ecology," p. 414.

43. See Stoltenberg, *Politische Strömungen*, pp.
13ff. (pre-1914); pp. 30ff. (1919 election); pp.
116ff. (1928 election); pp. 163ff. (1930 election); and pp. 182ff. (1932 and 1933 elections).

44. Ibid., pp. 37-41, 78-80, 89, 116, and 118.

45. Ibid., pp. 48, 63, 100ff., 160.

46. Ibid., p. 48.

47. Ibid., p. 63.

48. Peter Wulf, *Die politische Haltung des
schleswig-holsteinischen Handwerks, 1928-32* (Köln
and Opladen, 1969), esp. pp. 35-36, 45, 77ff.

49. Ibid., p. 36.

50. Ibid., p. 83. [My emphasis.]

Chapter II: The Social Origins of Nazism in Rural
Schleswig-Holstein

    1.   Broder Christensen, *Hundert Jahre Bauern-
geschichte des Kreises Husum* (Husum, 1967), p. 43.
    2.   Christensen, *Hundert Jahre*, p. 42.
    3.   Hans Beyer, "Landbevölkerung in sich revo-
lutionär?" *Der Konvent*, Jg. 8, 1962, p. 74.
    4.   Christensen, *Hundert Jahre*, p. 40.
    5.   Thyge Thyssen, *Bauer und Standesvertretung:
Werden und Wirken des Bauerntums in Schleswig-
Holstein seit der Agrarreform* (Neumünster, 1958),
p. 484.
    6.   See the detailed discussion in Heberle,
Landbevölkerung, pp. 120-124.
    7.   Heberle, *From Democracy to Nazism*, p. 85.
    8.   Heberle, *Landbevölkerung*, pp. 74, 76.
    9.   Bodo Uhse, *Söldner und Soldat* (Frankfurt,
1967), pp. 153, 289, 156. Many disputed the wealthy
west-coast farmers' claim that they had suffered
serious economic hardship—the Social Democrats who
suspected the claims of an agrarian ruling class,
the representatives of the Berlin police who
reported that most Dithmarschen farmers could pay
their taxes if they would cut their high standard of
living a bit (Landesarchiv 301/4695 "Landvolkbewegung" and 309/22668 "Landvolk und Bauernunruhen"),
and the Frankfurt reporter who observed "surprising
collections of products of luxury industries—not to
speak of the ownership of large private automobiles." (*Frankfurter Zeitung*, #220, 23.3.1929).   In
mid-1929 *Der Landbote*, a farm paper, carried a
report on a meeting of distressed farmers; two
hundred and fifty people were present—and forty
automobiles. "The contributions flowed abundantly."
(*Der Landbote*, #41, 26.5.1929).
    10.   Stoltenberg, *Politische Strömungen*, p. 199.
    11.   Marquis Childs, *Sweden: The Middle Way*
(New Haven, 1947), p. 139.
    12.   On the "Self-Administration Movement" see
Troels Fink, *Geschichte des schleswigschen Grenz-
landes* (Copenhagen, 1958), pp. 209-216, and Hans
Beyer, "Der Friese Cornelius Petersen und der Land-
volkbewegungen zwischen den beiden Weltkriegan,"
Zeitschrift für Agrargeschichte und Agrarsoziologie,
Jg. 20, 1962, pp. 212-230.
    13.   See Fink, *Geschichte*, pp. 272-279.
    14.   Childs, *Sweden*, pp. 152-154; Jörgen
Weibull, "Sweden 1918-1968," a lecture delivered 12

December 1968 at University College, London, pp.
10-11.

15.   Sten Nilson, "Wahlsoziologische Probleme
der Nationalsozialismus," *Zeitschrift für die
gesamte Staatswissenschaft*, Vol. 110, 1954, pp.
300-301.

16.   Ibid., pp. 296-297.

17.   Ibid., p. 302.

18.   Ibid., p. 305.

19.   Barrington Moore, Jr., *Political Power and
Social Theory* (New York, 1962), p. 7.

20.   Stoltenberg, *Politische Strömungen*, p. 111.

21.   Hans Beyer, "Das Bauerntum Angelns während
der Grossen Krise 1926-1932," *Jahrbuch des Angler
Heimatvereins*, 1962, pp. 140-141.

22.   *Husumer Nachrichten*, 30 January 1928;
reproduced in Christensen, *Hundert Jahre*, p. 36.

23.   Ibid., p. 37.

24.   Landesarchiv 301/4695. Johannsen's report
of 3 March 1928.

25.   Hans Fallada, *Bauern Bomben und Bonzen*
(Berlin, 1931), p. 64.

26.   See the report of the *Frankfurter Zeitung*,
#20, 23 March 1929. Landesarchiv 309/22921.

27.   Ibid.

28.   See Heberle, *Landbevölkerung*, p. 123 footnote.

29.   *Frankfurter Zeitung*, #220, 23 March 1929.

30.   Fallada, *Bauern*, p. 20.

31.   Thyge Thyssen, *Bauer*, p. 296.

32.   "My previous suspicion, that the organization 'Stahlhelm-Westküste' (Frontkämpferbund)
founded in the fall of 1924,...was linked in the
closest possible way with the Landvolk movement was
confirmed by the confiscated material. Hamkens,
Heim, Nickels, and Volck were prominent members of
the Stahlhelm Westküste." Landesarchiv 301/4696.
For further material on these predecessors of the
Nazis see Heberle, *From Democracy to Nazism*, p. 57,
and Stoltenberg, *Politische Strömungen*, pp. 49ff.,
78ff., and 97ff.

33.   Landesarchiv 301/4695. The meeting was
held on 11 November 1928.

34.   Heberle, *From Democracy to Nazism*, pp. 49-
50. "The freedom-loving, soil-rooted population,
particularly on the west coast, now often considered
the earlier situation, under which they determined
their own laws and conducted their own administration, as superior to present-day conditions....The

experiences of the past years have now shown them
that the farmers cannot achieve the restructuring of
their situation that they consider necessary either
through the parties to which they have previously
entrusted the representation of their essential
interests or through their own self-created and
self-elected interest organizations." Landesarchiv
301/4690.

35.   Cf. Daniel Bell, "The Dispossessed," in *The
Radical Right*, ed. Daniel Bell (New York, 1964), p.
16: "What the right wing is fighting, in the shadow
of Communism, is essentially 'modernity'—that
complex of attitudes that might be defined most
simply as the belief in rational assessment, rather
than established custom for the evaluation of social
change—and what it seeks to defend is its fading
dominance, exercised once through the institutions
of small-town America, over the control of social
change." Peter Wulf describes a similar phenomenon
among rural craftsmen in *Die politische Haltung des
schleswig-holsteinischen Handwerks 1928-1932* (Köln
and Opladen, 1969), p. 46.

36.   Thyssen, *Bauer und Standesvertretung*, p.
295. For similar feelings among *Handwerker*, see
Wulf, *Haltung*, pp. 53ff. and *passim*.

37.   Stoltenberg, *Politische Strömungen*, p. 49.

38.   Cited in Klemens von Klemperer, *Germany's
New Conservatism: Its History and Dilemma in the
Twentieth Century* (Princeton, 1957).

39.   Heberle, *From Democracy to Nazism*, pp. 45-
62, gives a good discussion of the activities and
impact of these organizations.

40.   Beyer, "Das Bauerntum Angelns," p. 156.

41.   Fink, *Geschichte*, pp. 219ff.; Clausen,
Aufbau der Demokratie, pp. 47, 52. For an example
of the romantic nationalist nonsense that found a
home in rural areas, see Johannes Tonnesen, "Volk
und Boden: Ein Beitrag zur Bauernbewegung," *Fest-
gabe Anton Schifferer* (Breslau, 1931).

42.   See Wulf, *Haltung*, p. 37.

43.   *Historische Beiträge*, pp. 104ff., 113ff.
and Stoltenberg, *Politische Strömungen*, p. 66.
Heberle's assertion that prewar levels were rapidly
reattained (*Landbevölkerung*, p. 119) appears unwar-
ranted in light of the statistics.

44.   For a detailed examination of indebtedness
and interest burdens, see Heberle, *Landbevölkerung*,
pp. 120-124. For the immediate political consequences of the inflation settlement, see Stolten-

berg, *Politische Strömungen*, pp. 67ff.

45. Stoltenberg, *Politische Strömungen*, pp.
61-65.

46. Ibid., p. 97.

47. Hans Beyer, *Die Agrarkrise und die Landvolkbewegung in den Jahren 1928-1932: Ein Beitrag
zur Geschichte "revolutionärer" Bauernbewegungen
zwischen den beiden Weltkriegen* (Itzehoe, 1962),
p. 9.

48. Accounts of this meeting vary considerably.
Publicists of the Right later contended that the
farmers' representatives had been the victims of
shabby treatment. See Walter Luetgebrune, *Neu-
Preussens Bauernkrieg: Entstehung und Kampf der
Landvolkbewegung* (Hamburg, Berlin, Leipzig, 1931),
pp. 15-18; Jürgen Schimmelreiter (pseud.), *Unter der
schwarzen Bauernfahnen: Die Landvolkbewegung im
Kampfe für Deutschlands Befreiung* (Munich, 1929),
pp. 12-13; Richard Schapke, *Aufstand der Bauern*
(Leipzig, 1933), pp. 25ff.; Beyer, "Das Bauerntum
Angelns," p. 137.

49. Thyssen, *Bauer und Standesvertretung*, p.
376; Fink, *Geschichte*, p. 254.

50. Hans Beyer, "Die Landvolkbewegung
Schleswig-Holsteins und Niedersachsens 1928-1932,"
*Jahrbuch der Heimatgemeinschaft des Kreises Eckern-
förde*, 15 Jg., 1957, p. 179.

51. Thyssen, *Bauer und Standesvertretung*, p.
374.

52. Landesarchiv 301/4695.

53. Beyer, *Agrarkrise*, p. 11.

54. *Der Landbote*, Nr. 41, 26 May 1929. LA
309/22668. For the flavor of these trials, see
further Luetgebrune, *Neu-Preussens Bauernkrieg*.

55. Fallada, *Bauern*, pp. 151-152.

56. Consider the speech of Fallada's Vadder
Benthin, modeled on the speeches of *Landvolk*
leaders:

"Farmers of Pomerania, I say to you that we
have allowed our flag to be taken from us because we
are obedient to our beloved government. Because we
allow them to take everything away from us. Our
brother Reimer they have taken from us and today
they led Röhwer away to the hoosgow. Cattle and
horses they take right from the stalls. They seize
the harvest while it's still on the stalk and drive
us off our farms."

"Well, you ask, why do we permit that? Don't
we have representatives? local representatives?

state representatives? Reichstag deputies? a
Chamber of Agriculture and a German Agriculture
Council? Why don't they defend us? Why don't they
cry out in protest?"

"Fellow farmers, they have cried out in
protest. When they are here. But then they go to
Berlin. And then they return. And suddenly everything is different. We have to see, we have to
realize, that things cannot go as we had thought.
And that there must be taxes and still more taxes."

Pay the taxes, Benthin says, let them take your
cattle: "The fewer you have the smaller your tax
burden will be. And when you have nothing left at
all, then our beloved government will take care of
you, just as they have taken care of your parents,
who had saved up a couple thousand and who now go to
the welfare office and who have acquired a distinguished title for themselves: Welfare Recipient
(*Sozialrentner*)!"

"Pay your taxes till they bleed you white, I
tell you, till you can't pay any more, till they've
sucked all the marrow out of your bones, till you're
half starved. Then our dear government in Berlin
won't give you any more trouble, then you are
saved...." Fallada, *Bauern*, pp. 197-198.

57.   Landesarchiv 301/4556.

58.   Police Report on Kreis Steinburg, 28 March
1929. Landesarchiv 309/22921.

59.   Landesarchiv 309/22668.

60.   Ibid.

61.   Ibid.

62.   Ibid.

63.   Hinrich Lohse, Gauleiter, in *Schleswig-
Holsteinische Tageszeitung*, #2, 3 January 1932.

64.   Landesarchiv 301/4560; *Niekammer's Landwirtschaftliche Güter-Adressbücher, Band XXI:
Schleswig-Holstein* (Leipzig, 1927).

65.   "Rundschreiben Nr. 45," Landesarchiv
301/4560.

66.   Thyssen, *Bauer und Standesvertretung*,
p. 395.

67.   Wulf, *Haltung*, p. 98. Cf. also p. 26.

68.   Klaus Schwieger, "Das Ende der Weimarer
Republik in Süderdithmarschen," in Nis R. Nissen
(ed.), *Süderdithmarschen 1581-1970* (Heide, 1970),
pp. 188-196, gives a detailed account of Nazi
terror in one *Kreis*.

69.   William Kornhauser, *The Politics of Mass
Society* (Glencoe, 1959), p. 223.

70.   Ibid., p. 136.

Chapter III: Changes in the Political Infrastructure, 1933-1970

1.   Franz Osterroth, *Hundert Jahre*, p. 115.
2.   Troels Fink, *Geschichte des schleswigschen Grenzlandes* (Copenhagen, 1958), p. 295, relates the futility of Schleswig's Danish minority's abstaining from Nazi referenda.
3.   Alexandre and Margarete Mitscherlich, *Die Unfähigkeit zu trauern* (Munich, 1967), have some suggestive comments on the psychological processes involved in avoiding a sense of personal responsibility.
4.   *Beiträge zur historischen Statistik Schleswig-Holsteins*, hrsg. vom Statistischen Landesamt Schleswig-Holstein (Kiel, 1967), p. 10.
5.   *Die Flüchtlinge in Schleswig-Holstein*, Sonderheft F of the *Statistischen Monatshefte Schleswig-Holstein*, p. 12.
6.   Ibid., p. 18.
7.   On these problems, see Else Bohnsack, *Flüchtlinge und Einheimische in Schleswig-Holstein* (Kiel, 1956) pp. 76ff.; Friedrich Edding, *Die wirtschaftlich Eingliederung der Vertriebenen und Flüchtlinge in Schleswig-Holstein* (Berlin, 1955) pp. 35-44, 105; and Lenchen Rehders, *Probsteierhagen, Feifbergen und Gut Salzau: 1945-1950* (Kiel, 1953), *passim*.
8.   According to *Statistiches Handbuch für Schleswig-Holstein 1951*, p. 567.
9.   Cited in Heinz-Josef Varain, *Parteien und Verbände* (Köln and Opladen, 1964), p. 13.
10.   *Kieler Neueste Nachrichten*, 2 December 1941, cited in Edding, *Eingliederung*, p. 34.
11.   Rehders, *Flüchtlinge*, p. 58.
12.   Edding, *Eingliederung*, summarizes the arguments on p. 68.
13.   The standard work on the "land reform" in Schleswig-Holstein is Friedrich Boyens, *Siedlung und Bodenreform als Aufgabe des Bundes* (Hamburg, 1950). See also Edding, *Eingliederung*, pp. 68-79; *Topographischer Atlas Schleswig-Holsteins*, p. 84; and for the conservative case by a former director of the Landwirtschaftskammer, Thyge Thyssen, *Bauer und Standesvertretung*, pp. 526-537.
14.   Ulrich Matthée, *Elitenbildung in der kommunalen Politik: Eine Untersuchung über die Zirkulation der politischen Führungsgruppen am Beispiel des Kreises Segeberg. Dissertation* (Kiel, 1967).

15. Ibid., p. 144.
16. *Beiträge*, p. 82.
17. Ibid.
18. Landwirtschaftskammer Schleswig-Holstein,
*Die Produktionsstruktur in der schleswig-holstein-
ischen Landwirtschaft* (Kiel, 1967).
19. Emil Meyer, "Die landwirtschaftlichen
Betriebe in Schleswig-Holstein," *Statistische
Monatshefte Schleswig-Holstein*, 13.Jg., Heft 4
(April 1961), p. 79.
20. *Statistische Monatshefte Schleswig-
Holstein*, 19.Jg., Heft 6 (June 1967), p. 141.
21. Thyssen, *Bauer und Standesvertretung*,
p. 539.
22. Heberle, *Landbevölkerung*, p. 41.
23. Ernst Schoof, "Dithmarschen vor und nach
1945," in Nissen, *Süderdithmarschen 1581-1970*, pp.
197-204.
24. In Schleswig-Holstein this nationalist mood
included measures to curb Danish influences in the
party and a resolution calling for the firing of
workers and officials who voted for the Danish party.
For the SPD's tawdry record—a striking contrast to
its brave and noble actions on the Danish border
question after 1918—see Hermann Clausen, *Der Aufbau
der Demokratie in der Stadt Schleswig nach den zwei
Weltkriegen: Erinnerungen* (Flensburg, 1966), pp.
225-226, 275. It should be pointed out, however,
that these intense national sentiments may have
reduced the chances for radical nationalist parties
to obtain wide working-class support.
25. See especially Theodor Steltzer, *Sechzig
Jahre Zeitgenosse* (Munich, 1966), p. 182, 186ff.
26. Ibid., p. 105.
27. Ibid., p. 119.
28. Cited in Franz Neumann, *Der Block der
Heimatvertriebenen und Entrechteten 1950-1960: Ein
Beitrag zur Geschichte und Struktur einer politischen Interessenpartei* (Marburg, 1966), p. 27.
The account of the BHE relies largely on this
detailed work, but also on Martin Virchow, "Der
GB/BHE....Ein neuer Parteientyp?" *Parteien in der
Bundesrepublik: Studien zur Entwicklung der
deutschen Parteien bis zur Bundestagswahl 1953*
(Stuttgart and Düsseldorf, 1953), pp. 450-467.
29. Neumann, *BHE*, p. 380.
30. Ibid., p. 296.
30. Ibid., p. 296.
31. Ibid., p. 318.

32.   Ibid., p. 292.

33.   Ibid., p. 63.

34.   Ibid., p. 38.

35.   Ibid., p. 132.

36.   The BHE, Neumann estimates, got 72 percent
of the refugees' votes in the 1950 *Landtag* election
in Schleswig-Holstein. In 1953 they won about 41
percent and in 1958 only 25 percent. Social and
economic integration leading to a growing consciousness of themselves as workers or as property owners
rather than as refugees explains most of the decline
in the BHE vote. Ibid., p. 305.

37.   Clausen, *Der Aufbau*, p. 178.

38.   Ibid., p. 179.

39.   Fink, *Geschichte*, p. 325.

40.   Gerhard Isbary, *Problemgebiete in Spiegel
politischer Wahlen am Beispiel Schleswigs* (Bad
Godesberg, 1960), p. 11. M. Rainer Lepsius's treatment of the SSW in his essay on *Extremer Nationalismus* (Stuttgart, 1966), pp. 17ff., is internally
inconsistent and at variance with the facts.

41.   Isbary, *Problemgebiete*, p. 11.

42.   See Hans Georg Wieck, *Die Entstehung der
CDU und die Wiedergründung des Zentrums in Jahre
1945* (Düsseldorf, 1953), p. 44.

43.   Ibid., p. 155.

44.   Gerhard Schulz, "Die CDU—Merkmale ihres
Aufbaus," *Parteien in der Bundesrepublik*, p. 61.

45.   For the descriptions of the CDU groups see
Wieck, *Die Entstehung*, pp. 156ff., 165ff., 172ff.,
177ff., 180, 219. Schulz, "Die CDU" and Kurt
Jürgensen, *Die Gründung des Landes Schleswig-
Holstein nach dem zweiten Weltkrieg* (Neumünster,
1969) add little to this excellent account.

46.   Steltzer, *Sechzig Jahre Zeitgenosse*,
p. 186.

47.   Ibid.

48.   Cited in Jürgensen, *Die Gründung*, pp. 74-
75.

49.   Part of the CDU gain is illusory and is due
to the emigration of SPD- or BHE-voting refugees
rather than to the recruiting of new CDU voters.

50.   Heinz Sahner, "Die NPD in der Landtagswahl
vom 23.4.1967 in Schleswig-Holstein," in Scheuch,
Klingemann, Herz, ed., *Die NPD in den Landtagswahlen
1966-1968* (Köln, 1969), p. 46.

51.   Sahner, *Die NPD*, p. 89.

52.   The CDU vote varies with age and sex as
well. The 4 percent electoral samples show clearly

that a greater percentage of women than men vote for
the CDU (see Table III-5). In 1961, 1962, 1967, and
1969, for example, a plurality of male voters chose
the SPD and women's votes provided the margin of
victory for the CDU. The feminine preference for
the CDU is most marked among older women, and to a
lesser extent among women under thirty; this pattern
has persisted over time, suggesting that age—or
rather the experience of people at a certain state
in life—does make a political difference.

  53. On the fading of the *Rathausparteien*, see
Werner Grundmann, *Die Rathausparteien* (Göttingen,
1960) and Ulrich Matthée, *Elitenbildung, passim*.

  54. See Günther Franz, *Die politischen Wahlen
in Niedersachsen 1867-1949* (Bremen-Horn, 1953).
Also Hermann Meyn, *Die Deutsche Partei* (Düsseldorf,
1965) and Rudolf Holzgräber, "Die Deutsche Partei—
Partei eines neuen Konservatismus?" in *Parteien in
der Bundesrepublik*, on which accounts this brief
summary is based.

  55. Program for Second Bundestag, cited in
Holzgräber, "Die DP," p. 445.

  56. Meyn, *Die Deutsche Partei*, p. 44.

  57. In *Kreis* Stormarn in July 1950, the execu-
tive committees of the CDU, the FDP, and the DP
demanded the merger of these parties at the *Land*
level, and in *Kreis* Lauenburg their dissolution and
the formation of a new party by September 1 at the
latest was announced. Schulz, "Die CDU," p. 106.

  58. The best work on the SRP is Otto Büsch and
Peter Furth, *Rechtsradikalismus im Nachkriegsdeutschland: Studien über die "Sozialistische
Reichspartei" (SRP)* (Berlin and Frankfort, 1957), on
which the following account is based.

  59. Ibid., p. 73.
  60. Ibid., p. 76.
  61. Ibid., p. 98.
  62. Ibid., p. 155.
  63. The party won 7.2 percent of the vote in
Herzogtum Lauenburg, 4.5 percent in Schleswig, 3.9
percent in Norderdithmarschen, 3.7 percent in Eutin,
2.5 percent in Oldenburg, 2.2 percent in Lubeck, 2.1
percent in Stormarn, 1.3 percent in Eiderstedt, 1.2
percent in Neumünster, Husum, and Rendsburg, 1 percent in Plön and Eckernförde, 0.8 percent in Steinburg, 0.4 percent in Flensburg-Land, 0.1 percent in
Segeberg and Südtondern.

  64. Büsch and Furth, *Rechtsradikalismus*, p. 88.
The figures come from the party's own records.

  65. Ibid., p. 175.

Chapter IV: The NPD in Electoral Politics

1.   Wolfgang Hirsch-Weber and Klaus Schütz, *Wähler und Gewählte: Eine Untersuchung der Bundestagswahlen 1953* (Berlin and Frankfort, 1957), p. 149.

2.   Günther Franz, *Die politischen Wahlen in Niedersachsen 1867-1949* (Bremen-Horn, 1953); Scheuch et al., *Die NPD in den Landtagswahlen 1966-1968* (Köln, 1969); François Goguel, *Géographie des élections française de 1870 à 1951* (Paris, 1951); Perry Howard, *Political Tendencies in Louisiana 1812-1952* (Baton Rouge, 1957).

3.   Interview with Gunther Flessner, president of the Landwirtschaftskammer and a prominent CDU politician.

4.   Enno Heeren, "Der Index der Einkaufspreise landwirtschaftlicher Betriebsmittel," *Statistische Monatshefte*, Jg. 20, Nr. 1, January 1968, p. 16.

5.   *Die Zeit*, 26 April 1968.

6.   *Stormärner Tageblatt*, 9 March 1967.

7.   *Husumer Nachrichten*, 5 May 1968.

8.   Interview with Martin Matthiessen.

9.   *Husumer Nachrichten*, 23 September 1969.

10.   *Flensburger Tageblatt*, 1 September 1969.

11.   Nor are these regional concentrations located in the poorest areas of Schleswig-Holstein. The correlation between low income per capita and NPD voting in seventeen *Kreise* is insignificant ($-.02$ in 1967, $+.13$ in 1969).

12.   Sahner, "Die NPD in der Landtagswahl," p. 61.

13.   Ibid., pp. 65-67.

14.   Klaus Liepelt, "Anhänger der neuen Rechtspartei," *Politische Vierteljahresschrift*, Jg. 8, Nr. 2, 1968, p. 244.

15.   Heinz Sahner, *Politische Tradition, Sozialstruktur und Parteiensystem in Schleswig-Holstein* (Meisenheim am Glan, 1972), pp. 48, 137, 138. Nagle's careful study at the national level similarly discounts the thesis of strong refugee susceptibility to the NPD. John Nagle, *The National Democratic Party* (Berkeley, 1970), p. 141.

16.   Interview with Karl-Ernst Lober.

17.   *Die Welt*, 4 November 1968.

18.   Reinhard Kühnl, Rainer Rilling, Christine Sager, *Die NPD, Struktur, Ideologie und Funktion einer neofaschistischen Partei* (Frankfurt am Main, 1969), p. 290.

19. Figures provided by the Landwirtschaftskammer Schleswig-Holstein.

20. Landwirtschaftskammer Schleswig-Holstein,
Die Produktionsstruktur in der schleswig-holsteinis-
chen Landwirtschaft: Regionale Aspekte und Konse-
quenzen (Kiel, 1969), p. 18. Herr Dr. Wittern of
the Landwirtschaftskammer estimated that about 60
percent of the present debt load can be considered
investment; the remainder results from poor farming
or excessive consumption. (Interview 14 May 1970.)

21. Figures provided by the Landwirtschaftskammer Schleswig-Holstein.

22. Figures from the Statisches Landesamt
Schleswig-Holstein.

23. Anyone who doubts the validity of interviewing rural people about the votes of their neighbors fails to appreciate the nature of rural *Gemein-*
schaften in Schleswig-Holstein and might profitably
consult Hans-Dieter Klingemann's *Bestimmungsgründe*
der Wahlentscheidung im Bundestags-Wahlkreis Heil-
bronn (Meisenheim am Glan, 1969), p. 65, where
Klingemann reports that in southern German towns
with populations under 2,000, 59 percent of the
respondents said that six or more people knew how
they had voted.

24. "The electoral success of the CDU depends
to a high degree upon the readiness of the farm
leadership group to present itself as candidates."
Matthée, *Elitenbildung*, p. 64. In a comparative
study of two structurally similar south German
villages, one with a strong NPD following, the other
without, Ulrike Waller-Albrecht of Mannheim found
personal prestige and influence to be the decisive
explanatory factor.

25. Interview with Peter Jäger.

26. *Ost-Holsteinisches Tageblatt*, 19 April
1967.

27. See *Volkszeitung*, 25 March 1967.

28. In interview after interview one heard this
phrase or slight variations upon it.

29. For a detailed analysis see Landwirtschaftskammer, *Die Produktionsstruktur*, pp. 11 ff.

30. See *Beiträge*, pp. 96-97, 113 ff.

Chapter V: Nazi Success and NPD Failure in Rural
Schleswig-Holstein: Conclusions

1. Reinhard Kühnl, Rainer Rilling, Christine
Sager, *Die NPD. Struktur, Ideologie und Funktion*

einer neofaschistischen Partei (Frankfurt am Main, 1969).

2. Ibid., p. 11.

3. *Historische Beiträge*, pp. 82,81.

4. "The most effective theme of [Nazi] propaganda increasingly became the allusion to the coming 'Third Reich,' in which the farmers as 'the First Estate' would finally be freed of their distress and held in proper esteem." Stoltenberg, *Politische Strömungen*, p. 169.

5. Ibid., p. 117.

6. For a similar analysis see Maurice Duverger, "Sociologie des parties politique," in Georges Gurvitch (ed.), *Traité de sociologie* (Paris, 1960), pp. 30-31. "This political combat is also of a military character. The members of the Fascist militias pursue a training similar to that of a soldier. They learn to wear a uniform, to salute, to march, to handle arms, to fight; they are taught how to sabotage a meeting or struggle against enemy saboteurs, how to attack the headquarters of a party or a union, how to bludgeon the enemy, how to conduct street warfare. A Fascist party is essentially a kind of private army...."

7. Heberle, *From Democracy to Nazism*, p. 84.

8. Steltzer, *Sechzig Jahre Zeitgenosse*, p. 101.

9. *Beiträge zur historischen Statistik*, p. 82, 81. For all their propaganda about the virtues of peasant life, the Nazis did not keep men "down on the farm," but presided over a further emigration from the countryside. Taking urban employment is not an automatic innoculation against Fascism; the rural exiles could still vote NPD, but there is cogent evidence that this development does not occur: (1) Working-class areas of large cities give the NPD minute support; (2) Rural interviews indicate very few commuters who vote NPD.

10. Thyssen, *Bauer und Standesvertretung*, p. 298.

11. "A person identifies himself all the more firmly with a special grouping if his personal welfare appears to be tied up with the welfare of that group. The possibility of bettering his own situation—or at least the increased opportunity to improve the prospects of his children—tends to loosen the ties that bind him to a huge socio-occupational stratum...." Raymond Aron, *Progress and Disillusion* (New York, 1968), p. 11. Cf. also

p. 44 where Aron distinguishes collective and
individual liberation.

    12. The contrast with a genuinely historical
analysis like Karl Bracher's *The German Dictatorship*
is striking. Bracher offers a careful survey of the
similarities and differences between the Bonn and
Weimar republics, noting areas like Central Franconia where the NPD has succeeded in former Nazi
strongholds, but also citing instances where the
radical right now faces a much more difficult
assignment; e.g., in the universities. Bracher
further suggests that intervening social changes
have weakened the immunity of Catholic and Socialist
voters to the radical right and that the prospects
of the NPD have been increased by the influx of the
expellees and the change in the character of the
German army (in the Weimar period, Bracher writes,
professional soldiers were supposed to be unpolit-
ical). Bracher's analytic technique is admirable,
though one may differ (as I do) with his estimate of
the forces weakening resistance to the NPD. Karl
Bracher, *The German Dictatorship* (New York, 1970),
pp. 469-501.

Bibliography

I. *General Bibliographies*

Hector, Kurt. "Sammelbericht Schleswig-Holstein
    1960-1963." *Blätter für deutsche Landesge-
    schichte*, 100 Jg. (1964), pp. 612-641.
_____. "Schleswig-Holstein 1964-1967."
    Blätter für deutsche Landesgeschichte, 104 Jg.
    (1968), pp. 335-390.
Varain, Heinz. *Schleswig-Holstein 1918-1957: Eine
    politische Bibliographie*. Kiel, 1958.

II. *Electoral Statistics and Other Statistical
Material*

For the Weimar Republic the most valuable
source for electoral results in Schleswig-Holstein
is the set of hand-written tables in Rudolf
Heberle's manuscript for *Landbevölkerung und
Nationalsozialismus*. These tables, available at the
Institut für Zeitgeschichte in Munich, give results
by *Gemeinde*, whereas the volumes in the *Statistik
des deutschen Reiches* give results only by the much
larger Weimar electoral districts.

For the postwar period the following publications are relevant:

*Die Landeswahlen in Schleswig-Holstein vom 20. April
    1947*. Kiel: Herausgegeben vom Landeswahl-
    leiter für Schleswig-Holstein unter Mitwirkung
    des Statistischen Landesamtes, 1947.
*Die Kommunalwahlen in Schleswig-Holstein am 24.
    Oktober 1948*. *Statistische Monatshefte
    Schleswig-Holstein*, Sonderheft B. Kiel:
    Herausgegeben vom Statistischen Landesamt
    Schleswig-Holstein, n.d.
*Die Wahl zum ersten Bundestag in Schleswig-Holstein
    am 14. August 1949*. *Statistische Monatshefte
    Schleswig-Holstein*, Sonderheft D. Kiel:

171

Herausgegeben vom Statistischen Landesamt
Schleswig-Holstein, 1950.

*Gemeindestatistik Schleswig-Holstein Nr. 1: Wahl-
statistik:* Kiel-Wik: Herausgegeben vom
Statistischen Landesamt Schleswig-Holstein,
1950. (Results of Landeswahlen 1947, Kommunal-
und Kreistagswahlen 1948, Bundestagswahlen
1949, and Landtagswahlen 1950 by *Gemeinden*.)

*Sonderdienst des Statistischen Landesamtes Schles-
wig-Holstein 1950: Reihe Wahlen.* 7-80-3.
Kiel, 1950.

*Die Kreistagswahlen in Schleswig-Holstein 29. April
1951. Statistische Monatshefte Schleswig-
Holstein,* Nr. 3-5/51. Kiel, 1951, p. 15, in
*Statistische Beilage zum Amtsblatt für Schles-
wig-Holstein,* Nr. 24.

*Sonderdienst des Statistischen Landesamtes Schles-
wig-Holstein 1951: Reihe Wahlen.* Kiel, 1951.
(Kreistags- und Gemeindewahlen am 29. April
1951.)

*Sonderdienst des Statistischen Landesamtes Schles-
wig-Holstein 1953: Reihe Wahlen.* 7-80-7.
Kiel, 1953.

*Sonderdienst des Statistischen Landesamtes Schles-
wig-Holstein 1954: Reihe Wahlen.* Kiel, 1954.
(*Gemeinde* results incomplete.)

*Statistische Berichte des Statistischen Landesamtes
Schleswig-Holstein: Reihe Wahlen.* 7-80-6.
Kiel, 1955.

*Statistik von Schleswig-Holstein: Die Bundestags-
wahl am 15. September 1957 in Schleswig-
Holstein,* Heft 24. Kiel: Herausgegeben vom
Statistischen Landesamt, 1958.

*Statistische Berichte des Statistischen Landesamtes
Schleswig-Holstein 1957. B-III-1: Die Wahl
zum 3. Deutschen Bundestag am 15.9.1957 in
Schleswig-Holstein.* Kiel, 1957. (Complete
results by *Gemeinden* and *Stichprobe*.)

*Statistische Berichte des Statistischen Landesamtes
Schleswig-Holstein 1958. B-III-2: Landtags-
wahl.* Kiel, 1958. (Complete results by
Gemeinden and *Stichprobe* for *Landtagswahl* 28.
Sept. 1958.)

*Statistik von Schleswig-Holstein: Die Landtagswahl
am 28. September 1958 in Schleswig-Holstein,*
Heft 28. Kiel: Herausgegeben vom Statistisch-
en Landesamt Schleswig-Holstein, 1959.

*Statistische Berichte des Statistischen Landesamtes
Schleswig-Holstein 1959. B-III-2ff.: Kreis-
tagswahl.* Kiel, 1959.

*Statistische Berichte des Statistischen Landesamtes
    Schleswig-Holstein 1961. B-III: Die Bundes-
    tagswahl am 17. Sept. 1961.* Kiel, 1961.
    (Complete *Gemeinde* results and *Stichprobe*.)
*Statistische Berichte des Statistischen Landesamtes
    Schleswig-Holstein. B-III: Die Landtagswahl
    am 23.9.1962 in Schleswig-Holstein*, Kiel, 1962.
*Statistische Berichte des Statistischen Landesamtes
    Schleswig-Holstein 1962. B-III-3-5: Kreis-
    tagswahl.* Kiel, 1962.
*Statistische Berichte des Statistischen Landesamtes
    Schleswig-Holstein 1965. B-III-1: Wahlen.*
    Kiel, 1965. (Complete *Gemeinde* results and
    Stichprobe for *Bundestagswahl* 19. Sept. 1965.)
*Statistische Berichte des Statistischen Landesamtes
    Schleswig-Holstein 1966. B-III-3-41: Kreis-
    tagswahl.* Kiel, 1966.
*Statistische Berichte des Statistischen Landesamtes
    Schleswig-Holstein 1967. B-III-2-5: Die Land-
    tagswahl am 23. April 1967 in Schleswig-
    Holstein.* Kiel, 1967. (Complete *Gemeinde*
    results and *Stichprobe*.)
*Statistische Berichte des Statistischen Landesamtes
    Schleswig-Holstein 1969. B-III-1-5: Die
    Bundestagswahl am 28. Sept. 1969 in Schleswig-
    Holstein.* Kiel, 1969. (Complete *Gemeinde*
    results and *Stichprobe*.)
*Beitrage zur historischen Statistik Schleswig-
    Holsteins.* Kiel: Hrsg. vom Statistischen
    Landesamt Schleswig-Holstein, 1967.
*Die Flüchtlinge in Schleswig-Holstein: Die Ergeb-
    nisse der Flüchtlingssondererhebung des Landes-
    sozialministers Schleswig-Holstein.* Bear-
    beiter: Wilhelm Tetzlaff. Sonderheft F der
    Statistischen Monatshefte Schleswig-Holstein.
    Kiel, 1950.
Gemeindestatistik Schleswig-Holstein 1960/61. Kiel:
    Hrsg. vom Statistischen Landesamt Schleswig-
    Holstein, 1963.
Statistisches Jahrbuch Schleswig-Holstein 1950— (to
    present). Kiel: Hrsg. vom Statistischen
    Landesamt Schleswig-Holstein, 1950ff.
Thiede, Gunther. *Regionale Unterschiede in der
    Arbeitsverfassung der schleswig-holsteinischen
    Landwirtschaft. Statistik von Schleswig-
    Holstein*, Heft 13. Kiel: Hrsg. vom Statistis-
    chen Landesamt Schleswig-Holstein, 1953.
Mohr, D. *Über die Betriebsorganisation der Land-
    wirtschaft in den Naturräumen Schleswig-
    Holsteins. Statistik von Schleswig-Holstein*,

Heft 20.   Hrsg. vom Statistischen Landesamt
Schleswig-Holstein, 1956.

III.   *Archival Materials and Newspapers*

A.   *Landesarchiv* (Schloss Gottorp, Schleswig)
  1.   Akten des Oberpräsidenten
       301/4555-4564   NSDAP 1925-1933
       301/4690-4691   Versammlungstätigkeit radi-
                       kaler Organisationen
       301/4695-4697   Landvolkbewegung
  2.   Akten des Regierungspräsidenten
       309/22668   Landvolkbewegung; Bauernunruhen
                   1929
       309/22669   Versammlungstätigkeit radikaler
                   Verbänden
       309/22696   Landvolk-, Junglandvolkbewegung;
                   Bauernunruhen Winter 1928-1929.
       309/22766   DNVP
       309/22789   Jungdeutscher Orden
       309/22921   Landvolk und Nothilfebewegung;
                   Bauernunruhen 1928-29
       309/22998   Standort der nationalsozia-
                   listischen Bewegung im
                   Regierungsbezirk
B.   *Archiv—Seminar für Geschichte und Wissenschaft
     der Politik*; Christian-Albrechts Universität,
     Kiel
          The *Seminar* maintains an extensive, indexed
     archive of clippings from the following news-
     papers.   During my stay in Kiel the entries for
     1957-63 and 1967-69 were available to me; those
     for 1964-66 were not available for use.
          Dithmarscher Landeszeitung
          Eckernförder Zeitung
          Eutiner Tageblatt
          Flensburger Tageblatt
          Husumer Nachrichten
          Kieler Nachrichten
          Lübecker Landeszeitung
          Lübecker Mittagsblatt
          Lübecker Nachrichten
          Neue Zürcher Zeitung
          Nordfriesische Nachrichten
          Oldenburger Heimat-Anzeiger
          Ostholsteinisches Tageblatt
          Pinneberger Tageblatt
          Schleswiger Nachrichten
          Schleswig-Holsteinische Landeszeitung

Stormarner Tageblatt
Volkszeitung
Die Welt
Die Zeit

C. *Landesbibliothek* (Kiel)
The *Landesbibliothek* has a complete file of
the regional Nazi newspaper, the *Schleswig-
Holsteinische Tageszeitung*.

IV. *Books and Articles*

Abendroth, Wolfgang. "Aufgaben und Methoden einer
deutschen historischen Wahlsoziologie," *Vier-
teljahresheft fur Zeitgeschichte*, Vol. 5
(1957), pp. 300-306.
Aron, Raymond. *Progress and Disillusion: The
Dialectics of Modern Society*. New York, 1968.
Bachem, Hans. "Radikale Parteien im demokratischen
System: Bedingungen für Erfolg oder Misser-
folg," *Aus Politik und Zeitgeschichte: Beilage
zur Wochenzeitung Das Parlament*, 6. Dezember
1967.
Beckmann, Fritz. "Der Bauer im Zeitalter des Kapi-
talismus," *Schmollers Jahrbuch*, 51 Jg. (1927),
pp. 49-91.
Bell, Daniel, ed. *The Radical Right*. New York,
1963.
Beyer, Hans. "Die Agrarkrise und das Ende der
Weimarer Republik" *Zeitschrift für Agrargeschichte und Agrarsoziologie*, 13 Jg. (1965),
pp. 62-92.
_____. *Die Agrarkrise und die Landvolkbewegung
in den Jahren 1928-1932: Ein Beitrag zur
Geschichte "revolutionärer" Bauernbewegungen
zwischen den beiden Weltkriegen*. Itzehoe,
1962.
_____. "Das Bauerntum Angelns während der
Grossen Krise 1927-1932," *Jahrbuch des Angler
Heimatvereins 1962*, pp. 131-161.
_____. "Der Friese Cornelius Petersen und
'Bondens Selvstyre': Ein dänisches Beispiel
für die Problematik der Landvolkbewegung
zwischen den beiden Weltkriegen," *Zeitschrift
für Agrargeschichte und Agrarsoziologie*, Jg. 10
(1962), pp. 212-230.
_____. *120 Jahre Landwirtschaftlicher Verein
für das südwestliche Holstein 1845-1965*.
Itzehoe, n.d.
_____. "Krempe in der Zeitgeschichte: Wand-

lungen einer 'bürgerlichen' Landstadt im 20.
Jahrhundert," *Steinburger Jahrbuch*, 8 Jg.
(1964), pp. 36-55.

_____. "'Landbevölkerung in sich revolu-
tionär'?" *Der Konvent* Jg. 8. Kiel, 1962, pp.
73-75.

_____. "Die Landvolkbewegung Schleswig-
Holsteins und Niedersachsens 1928-1932," *Jahrbuch der Heimatgemeinschaft des Kreises Eckernförde*, 15 Jg. (1957), pp. 173-202.

_____. "Verwaltung, politisches Leben und Wirt-
schaft im Kreise Oldenburg 1867-1967," *Jahrbuch
für Heimatkunde im Kreis Oldenburg-Holstein*,
Jg. 12 (1966), pp. 31-94.

_____. "Landbevölkerung und Nationalsozialis-
mus in Schleswig-Holstein," *Zeitschrift für
Agrargeschichte und Agrarsoziologie*, Jg. 12
(1964), pp. 69-74.

Bohnsack, Else. *Flüchtlinge und Einheimische in
Schleswig-Holstein*. Kiel, 1956. (I used
dissertation *Einheimische und Flüchtlinge* in
*Schleswig-Holstein: Ergebnisse einer Stich-
probenerhebung 1953*. Kiel, 1954.)

Böttger, Franz and Horst Weimann. *Siggen: Die
Geschichte eines ostholsteinischen Gutes*.
Lübeck, 1967.

Boyens, Wilhelm F. *Siedlung und Bodenreform als
Aufgabe des Bundes: Schleswig-Holsteins
Beitrag zur Frage der ländlichen Siedlung*.
Hamburg, 1950. (Schriftenreihe der Gesell-
schaft zur Förderung der Inneren Kolonisation,
Heft 1.)

Bracher, Karl D. *The German Dictatorship: The
Origins, Structure, and Effects of National
Socialism*. New York, 1970.

Bremme, Gabriele. *Die politische Rolle der Frau in
Deutschland: Eine Untersuchung über den
Einfluss der Frauen bei Wahlen und ihre Teil-
nahme in Partei und Parlament*. Göttingen,
1956.

Büsch, Otto and Peter Furth. *Rechtsradikalismus im
Nachkriegsdeutschland: Studien über die
"Sozialistische Reichspartei" (SRP)*. Berlin
and Frankfurt, 1957.

Childs, Marquis. *Sweden: The Middle Way*. New
Haven, 1947.

Christensen, Broder. *Hundert Jahre Bauerngeschichte
des Kreises Husum*. Husum, 1967.

Clausen, Hermann. *Der Aufbau der Demokratie in der Stadt Schleswig nach den zwei Weltkriegen.* Flensburg, 1966.

Conze, Werner. "Wahlsoziologie und Parteige-schichte: Neue französische Forschungen," *Aus Geschichte und Politik: Festschrift zum 70. Geburtstag von Ludwig Bergstraesser.* Hrsg. Alfred Herrmann. Düsseldorf, 1954, pp. 243-251.

Dirks, Walter. "Der restaurative Charakter der Epoche," *Frankfurter Hefte*, 5 Jg., Heft 9 (1950), pp. 942-954.

Edding, Friedrich. *Die wirtschaftliche Eingliede-rung der Vertriebenen und Flüchtlinge in Schleswig-Holstein.* Berlin, 1955.

Fallada, Hans. *Bauern Bonzen und Bomben.* Berlin, 1931. (Novel.)

Fink, Troels. *Geschichte des schleswigschen Grenz-landes.* Copenhagen, 1958.

Fink, Willibald. *Die NPD bei der Bayrischen Land-tagswahl 1966.* München, 1969.

Flechtheim, Ossip, ed. *Die deutschen Parteien seit 1945.* Berlin, 1955.

_____. "Das Dilemma des Konservatismus," *Gewerkschaftliche Monatshefte*, 14 Jg. (1963), pp. 83-89.

Flensburg Geschichte einer Grenzstadt. Flensburg, 1966.

Franz, Günther. *Die politischen Wahlen in Nieder-sachsen 1867-1949.* 2nd edition with supple-ment, "Die Wahlen 1951 und 1952." Bremen-Horn, 1953.

Friedrich, Carl J. "The Agricultural Basis of Emotional Nationalism," *Public Opinion Quar-terly*, Vol. 1, No. 2 (1937), pp. 50-61.

Gerschenkron, Alexander. *Bread and Democracy in Germany.* Berkeley, 1943.

Glismann, H. A. *Die Geschichte des Truppenübungs-platzes Lockstedter Lager und seine Entwicklung zum Industrieort Hohenlockstedt.* Itzehoe, 1962.

Goguel, François. *Géographie des élections fran-çaises de 1870 à 1951.* Paris, 1951.

_____. "La sociologie électorale," in Georges Gurvitch, ed., *Traité de Sociologie.* Paris, 1960, pp. 46-63.

Grundmann, Werner W. *Die Rathausparteien: Die rechtliche und faktische Stellung örtlich*

*begrenzter Wählerorganisationen bei den Kommu-
nalwahlen in der Bundesrepublik Deutschland.*
Göttingen, 1960.

Gusfield, Joseph. "Mass Society and Extremist Politics," *American Sociological Review*, Vol. 27,
No. 1 (1962), pp. 19-30.

Hannesen, Hans. *Die Agrarlandschaft der schleswig-
holsteinische Geest und ihre neuzeitliche Ent-
wickuung.* Kiel, 1959.

Heberle, Rudolf. "The Ecology of Political Parties:
A Study of Elections in Rural Communities in
Schleswig-Holstein, 1918-1932," *American Socio-
logical Review*, Vol. XI (1944), pp. 401-414.

_____. *From Democracy to Nazism: A Regional
Case Study on Political Parties in Germany.*
Baton Rouge, 1945, 1970.

_____. *Hauptprobleme der politischen Sozio-
logie.* Stuttgart, 1964.

_____. *Landbevölkerung und Nationalsozialis-
mus: Eine soziologische Untersuchung der
politischen Willensbildung in Schleswig-
Holstein 1918 bis 1932.* Stuttgart, 1963.

_____. "Die politische Haltung des Landvolks
in Schleswig-Holstein 1918-1932," *Volksspiegel*,
1 Jg., Nr. 4 (1934), pp. 166-172.

_____. "The Political Movements among the
Rural People in Schleswig-Holstein, 1918-1932,"
Journal of Politics, Vol. 5, No. 1, pp. 3-27,
and Vol. 5, No. 2, pp. 115-142 (1943).

_____. *Social Movements.* New York, 1951.

Hirsch-Weber, Wolfgang and Klaus Schütz. *Wähler und
Gewählte: Eine Untersuchung der Bundestagswahlen 1953.* Berlin and Frankfurt, 1957.

Holt, John B. *German Agricultural Policy 1918-1932:
The Development of a National Philosophy Toward
Agriculture in Postwar Germany.* Chapel Hill,
1936.

Irmisch, Rudolf. *Geschichte der Stadt Itzehoe.*
Itzehoe, 1960.

Isbary, Gerhard. *Problemgebiete im Speigel politischer Wahlen am Beispiel Schleswigs.* Bad
Godesberg, 1960.

Jürgensen, Kurt. *Die Gründung des Landes Schleswig-
Holstein nach dem zweiten Weltkrieg.*
Neumünster, 1969.

Kaase, Max. *Wechsel von Parteipräferenzen: Eine
Analyse am Beispiel der Bundestagswahl 1961.*
Meisenheim am Glan, 1967.

Kappe, Dieter. "Nationalismus und Demokratie:

Versuch einer Strukturanalyse der NPD,"
Hamburger Jahrbuch für Wirtschafts- und Gesell-
schaftspolitik. Ed. H. D. Ortlieb and Bruno
Molitor. Tübingen, 1967, pp. 30-44.

Kitzinger, Uwe. *German Electoral Politics: A Study*
of the 1957 Campaign. Oxford, 1960.

Klemperer, Klemens von. *Germany's New Conservatism:*
Its History and Dilemma in the Twentieth
Century. Princeton, 1957.

Klingemann, Hans-Dieter. *Bestimmungsgründe der Wahl-*
entscheidung im Bundestagswahlkreis Heilbronn.
Meisenheim am Glan, 1969.

_____ and Franz U. Pappi. *Politischer Radi-*
kalismus: Theoretische und methodische Prob-
leme der Radikalismusforschung, dargestellt am
Beispiel einer Studie anlässlich der Landtags-
wahl 1970 in Hessen. München, Wien, 1972.

Knütter, Hans-Helmuth. *Ideologien des Rechtsradi-*
kalismus im Nachkriegsdeutschland: Eine Studie
über die Nachwirkungen des Nationalsozialismus.
Bonn, 1961. (Originally *Das Bild des National-*
sozialismus in der Publizistik der radikalen
Rechten nach 1945: Eine Studie zum Problem der
Kontinuität und Anpassung Politischer Ideen, a
much more accurate title.)

Kornhauser, William. *The Politics of Mass Society.*
Glencoe, 1959.

Krautzpaul, Marthe. *Die soziale und berufliche*
Umschichtung der Vertriebenen, Flüchtlinge und
Evakuierten des Kreises Herzogtum Lauenburg
(Schleswig-Holstein) in den Jahren 1945/49.
Dissertation. Kiel, 1952.

Krickhahn, Wolfgang. "Die Wirtschaft im Kreis
Pinneberg," *Jahrbuch für den Kreis Pinneberg*
(1970), pp. 142-160.

Kühnl, Reinhard, Rainer Rilling, Christine Sager.
Die NPD. Struktur, Ideologie und Funktion
einer neofaschistischen Partei. Frankfurt,
1969.

_____. *Die NPD—Struktur, Programm und Ideo-*
logie einer neofaschistischen Partei. Berlin,
1967.

Landwirtschaft in Schleswig-Holstein: Ein Überblick
über Struktur und Entwicklung der landwirt-
schaftlichen Betriebe und ihrer Grundlagen.
Hrsg. im Ministerium für Ernährung, Landwirtschaft und Forsten des Landes Schleswig-
Holstein. Kiel, 1960.

Lepsius, M. Rainer. *Extremer Nationalismus: Struk-*

*turbedingungen vor der nationalsozialistischen
    Machtergreifung*. Stuttgart, 1966.
Loomis, Charles P. and J. Allan Beegle. "The Spread
    of German Nazism in Rural Areas," *American
    Sociological Review*, Vol. XIII (1946), pp. 724-
    734.
Luetgebrune, Walter. *Neu-Preussens Bauernkrieg:
    Entstehung und Kampf der Landvolkbewegung*.
    Hamburg, Berlin, Leipzig, 1931.
Matthée, Ulrich. *Elitenbildung in der kommunalen
    Politik: Eine Untersuchung über die Zirkula-
    tion der politischer Führungsgruppen am
    Beispiel des Kreises Segeberg*. Dissertation.
    Kiel, 1967.
Meyn, Hermann. *Die Deutsche Partei: Entwicklung
    und Problematik einer national-konservativen
    Rechtspartei nach 1945*. Düsseldorf, 1965.
Mitscherlich, Alexander and Margarete. *Die Unfähig-
    keit zu trauern*. München, 1967.
Mohler, Armin. *Die Konservative Revolution in
    Deutschland 1918-1932: Grundriss ihrer Welt-
    anschauungen*. Stuttgart, 1950.
Moore, Jr., Barrington. *Political Power and Social
    Theory*. New York, 1962.
_____. *Social Origins of Dictatorship and
    Democracy*. Boston, 1966.
Nagle, John David. *The National Democratic Party:
    Right Radicalism in the Federal Republic of
    Germany*. Berkeley, 1970.
Neumann, Franz. *Der Block der Heimatvertriebenen
    und Entrechteten 1950-1960: Ein Beitrag zur
    Geschichte und Struktur einer politischen
    Interessenpartei*. Marburg/Lahn, 1966.
*Niekammer's Landwirtschaftliche Güter—Adressbucher
    Band XXI: Schleswig-Holstein*. Hrsg. Dr. H.
    Kording und Hans Wehner. Leipzig, 1927.
Niethammer, Lutz. *Angepasster Faschismus: Poli-
    tische Praxis der NPD*. Frankfurt am Main,
    1969.
Nilson, Sten S. "Wahlsoziologische Probleme des
    Nationalsozialismus," *Zeitschrift für die
    gesamte Stattswissenschaft*, Vol. 110 (1954),
    pp. 279-311.
Nissen, Nis R., ed. *Süderdithmarschen 1581-1970*.
    Heide, 1970.
Die NPD in den Landtagswahlen 1966-1968. Hrsg.
    Erwin Scheuch, Hans Klingemann, Thomas Herz.
    Manuscript. Köln, 1969.
Osterroth, Franz. *Hundert Jahre Sozialdemokratie in*

Schleswig-Holstein. Kiel, 1963.

Parteien in der Bundesrepublik: Studien zur Entwicklung der deutschen Parteien bis zur Bundestagswahl 1953. Stuttgart und Düsseldorf, 1953.

Planungsatlas Schleswig-Holstein. Wissenschaftliche und kartographische Gesamtbearbeitung: Werner Witt. Bremen-Horn, 1960.

Die Produktionsstruktur in der schleswig-holstein-ischen Landwirtschaft: Regionale Aspekte und Konsequenzen. Hrsg. Landwirtschaftskammer Schleswig-Holstein. Kiel, 1969.

Rehders, Lenchen. *Probsteierhagen, Fiefbergen und Gut Salzau: 1945-1950, Wandlungen dreier ländlicher Siedlungen in Schleswig-Holstein durch den Flüchtlingszustrom, Schriften des Geographischen Instituts der Universität Kiel.* Kiel, 1953.

Sahner, Heinz. *Die NPD in der Landtagswahl 1967 in Schleswig-Holstein.* Diplomarbeit. Köln, 1969.

_____. "Die NPD in der Landtagswahl vom 23.4.1967 in Schleswig-Holstein," in *Die NPD in der Landtagswahlen 1966-1968* (ed. Erwin Scheuch, Hans Klingemann, Thomas Herz), Köln, 1969.

_____. *Politische Tradition, Sozialstruktur und Parteiensystem in Schleswig-Holstein* (*Politik und Tradition*, Band 9) Meisenheim am Glan, 1972.

Saposs, David. "The Role of the Middle Class in Social Development: Fascism, Populism, Communism, Socialism" *Economic Essays in Honor of Wesley Clair Mitchell.* New York, 1935, pp. 393-424.

Schapke, Richard. *Aufstand der Bauern.* Leipzig, 1933.

Scheuch, Erwin (unter Mitarbeit von Hans Klingemann), "Theorie des Rechtsradikalismus in westlichen Industriegesellschaften," *Hamburger Jahrbuch für Wirtschafts- und Gesellschaftspolitik.* Tübingen, 1967, pp. 11-29.

_____ and Rudolf Wildenmann, eds. *Zur Soziologie der Wahl. Kölner Zeitschrift für Soziologie und Sozialpsychologie*, Sonderheft 9 (1965). Köln and Opladen.

Schimmelreiter, Jürgen. *Unter der schwarzen Bauernfahne: Die Landvolkbewegung im Kampfe für Deutschlands Befreiung.* München, 1929. (Pseud. for an East Holstein school teacher and

            partisan of the movement.)
Schüddekopf, Otto-Ernst. *Linke Leute von rechts:
     Die national-revolutionären Minderheiten und
     der Kommunismus in der Weimarer Republik.*
     Stuttgart, 1960.
Sering, Max. *Erbrecht und Agrarverfassung in
     Schleswig-Holstein auf geschichtlicher Grund-
     lage.* Berlin, 1907.
Siegfried, André. *Tableau politique de la France de
     l'ouest sous la troisième république.* Paris,
     1913.
Steltzer, Theodor. *Sechzig Jahre Zeitgenosse.*
     München, 1966.
Stoltenberg, Gerhard. *Politische Strömungen im
     schleswig-holsteinischen Landvolk 1918-1933:
     Ein Beitrag zur politischen Meinungsbildung in
     der Weimarer Republik.* Düsseldorf, 1962.
Thyssen, Thyge. *Bauer und Standesvertretung:
     Werden und Wirken des Bauerntums in Schleswig-
     Holstein seit der Agrarreform.* Neumünster,
     1958.
Tonnensen, Johannes. "Volk und Boden: Ein Beitrag
     zur Bauernbewegung," *Festgabe Anton Schifferer.*
     Breslau, 1931, pp. 83-93.
Topographischer Atlas Schleswig-Holstein. Hrsg. vom
     Landesvermessungsamt Schleswig-Holstein.
     Neumünster, 1966.
Uhse, Bodo. *Söldner und Soldat.* Frankfurt, 1967.
Varain, Heinz-Josef. *Parteien und Verbände: Eine
     Studie über ihren Aufbau, ihrer Verflechtung
     und ihr Wirken in Schleswig-Holstein 1945-1958.*
     Köln and Opladen, 1964.
*Die Vertriebenen in Westdeutschland: Ihre Ein-
     gliederung und Ihr Einfluss auf Gesellschaft,
     Wirtschaft, Politik und Geistesleben.* Eugen
     Lemberg and Friedrich Edding, eds. 3 volumes.
     Kiel, 1959.
Vogel, Bernhard and Peter Haungs. *Wahlkampf und
     Wählertradition: Eine Studie zur Bundestags-
     wahl von 1961.* Köln and Opladen, 1965.
Volck, Herbert. *Rebellen um Ehre.* Berlin, 1932.
Weibull, Jorgen. "Sweden 1918-1968," a lecture
     delivered 12 December 1968 at University
     College, London.
Witt, Knut H. *Der Strukturwandel in Lütjenburg und
     seinem Nachbarschaftgebiet.* Plön, 1964.
Wulf, Peter. *Die politische Haltung des schleswig-
     holsteinischen Handwerks 1928-1932.* Köln and
     Opladen, 1969.

Index

Agricultural crisis, 39, 40, 41-47, 70, 142; structural, 1-3, 6, 79-80, 126-127, 136, 141, 142; cyclical, 41-47, 47-48 (Denmark), 49 (Norway), 113-114, 123, 136, 142

Agricultural policy, 2, 6, 14, 52, 53, 54, 60-62, 82, 113-114, 127, 128, 130, 136-137, 141

Albrecht-Waller, Ulrike, 6

Angeln, 25, 26, 27, 46, 67

Anti-Semitism, 16

Arbeitsgemeinschaft Dithmarschen, 55

Bauernverband, 113

Beyer, Hans, 7, 65-66

BHE (*Bund der Heimatvertriebenen und Entrechteten*), 86, 87, 88, 89, 91-96

CDU (*Christlich Demokratische Union*), 86, 87, 88, 89, 98-103, 112, 113, 131, 132, 142

Christensen, Broder, 39-40

Christian Democratic Union. *See* CDU

Class structure, 20-22, 24-25, 28-29, 30-31, 35-36, 49, 58-59, 79, 118-130, 135

Clausen, Herman, 11

Common Market, 113, 127

Communist Party of Germany. *See* KPD

Danish Question. *See* Denmark

DDP (*Deutsche Demokratische Partei*), 14, 18-19, 22, 28, 30, 32, 61

Denmark, 47-48, 58, 96-98, 142

Dithmarschen, 20, 21, 22, 25, 53-56, 62, 112, 126

DKP (*Deutsche Konservative Partei*), 106

DNVP (*Deutschnationale Volkspartei*), 16, 18-19, 22, 25, 26, 27, 29, 30, 32, 33, 34-35, 56, 61, 115

DP (*Deutsche Partei*), 104-105

DRP (*Deutsche Reichspartei*), 113

DVP (*Deutsche Volkspartei*), 14, 18-19, 26, 30, 32, 61

Ecology, political, 2-3, 5, 7-34, 37, 72, 82-85, 90-91, 101-103,

110-111, 117-121
Ehlers, Wolfgang, 112,
    127
Elections, 5, 7-8, 9-11,
    14, 16, 22, 23, 25-26,
    28-29, 34, 35-36, 37,
    61, 67, 73, 83, 84,
    101, 107, 111, 112,
    115-121
Emigration, rural, 1, 2,
    43, 45, 78, 80, 82,
    141-143

Farmers. *See Bauernver-
    band*, Farm interest
    organizations, Farm
    workers, Peasantry
Farm interest organiza-
    tions, 11, 58, 60-61,
    62, 68, 70-71, 113,
    136
Farm workers, 21, 23,
    24, 25, 28, 29, 31,
    33, 46, 58, 78, 80,
    91
Fascism, 1, 3, 4, 47,
    48, 95, 134, 142. *See
    also* Nazism, NSDAP
FDP (*Freie Demokratische
    Partei*), 86, 87, 88,
    89, 103-104
Free Democratic Party.
    See FDP

Geest, 12, 16, 18, 23,
    26-29, 67
German Conservative
    Party. *See* DKP
German Democratic Party.
    See DDP
German National People's
    Party. *See* DNVP
German Party. *See* DP
German People's Party.
    See DVP
German Reich Party. *See*
    DRP
Great Coalition, 113

Hansen, Hein, 46
Heberle, Rudolf, 2, 3,
    4, 5, 7-14, 16, 22-24,
    28, 29, 31, 33-34, 56,
    138
Hill area, 12, 19, 24-
    26, 91, 92
Historical comparison,
    110-111, 134-143

Indebtedness, 43, 48,
    50, 51, 52, 54, 60,
    123-126
Independent Social Demo-
    cratic Party. *See*
    USDP
Inflation, 52, 59
Iversen, Willi, 14

Jäger, Peter, 121-122
Johannsen, Adolf, 53, 62
Johannsen, Otto, 51-52,
    60, 61

Kapp putsch, 58, 59
Kehr, Hans, 114
KPD (*Kommunistische
    Partei Deutschlands*),
    12, 16, 18-19, 22, 25,
    27, 30, 32, 46, 85
Kraft, Waldemar, 93, 94,
    95
Kühnl, Reinhard, 123,
    126, 134, 143

Landespartei, 14-16, 18-
    19, 28, 30, 32, 58
Landvolk, 18-19, 30, 55,
    62-66, 69
Leadership, 24, 28, 67-
    68, 137-139
League of the Homeless
    and Disinherited. *See*
    BHE
Liberalism, 9-10, 11,
    14, 37
Lober, Karl-Ernst, 112
Local elections, 35-36,
    37

Local notables, 24, 25, 33, 46, 55, 56, 57, 59, 67, 68, 79, 127–129, 137. *See also* Personal influence
Lohse, Hinrich, 16

Marginal upper-class farmer, 1, 126–129
Marsh area, 12, 18, 20–24
Mass society, 70
Modernization, 1, 2, 79–83, 103, 139, 141–143
Moore, Barrington, 2, 51

Nagle, John, 6
National Democratic Party of Germany. *See* NPD
Nationalism, 34, 39, 52, 56, 58, 70, 95, 100, 101, 104, 112, 114, 115, 136, 140
National Socialist German Labor Party. *See* NSDAP
Nazism, 1, 2, 6, 73. *See also* NSDAP
Neo-Nazism, 3, 4, 115. *See also* NPD
Newspapers, 66, 114, 115, 130
Norway, 48–50
NPD (*Nationaldemokrat-isches Partei Deutsch-lands*), 1, 3, 4, 5, 6, 86, 87, 109, 110–143
NSDAP (*Nationalsozial-istische Deutsche Arbeiterpartei*), 1, 2, 5, 6, 8, 12, 13, 14, 16, 18–19, 22, 26, 27, 29, 30, 32, 33, 37, 40, 46, 55, 61, 62, 65, 66, 67–71, 115, 117, 134–139. *See also* Nazism

Oberfohren, Reichstag deputy, DNVP, 33
Organization, 35–37, 65, 67–69, 70, 132, 137–139

Party system, 83–109, 137
Peasantry, 1, 2, 6, 7, 9, 11, 20–21, 24–25, 26, 28–29, 30, 31, 40, 43, 45, 47, 49, 53, 59, 60, 61, 62, 63, 65, 68, 70–71, 76, 78, 79, 80, 102, 112, 113, 114, 123–127, 130, 132, 135, 137, 141
Personal influence, 127–129. *See also* Local notables
Petersen, Cornelius, 47–48
Petersen, Peter, 112
Political tradition, 9–11, 24, 25–26, 37, 41, 51, 56–58, 70, 131, 135–136, 140
Probstei, 25, 27
Progressive Party, 8–9

Reese, Heinrich, 52
Refugees, 73–78, 91, 93–96, 119
Rheingans, Uwe, 111, 112, 114
Right-wing extremism, 1, 3, 55–56, 60, 62–66, 105, 112, 142. *See also* Neo-Nazism, NPD

Sahner, Heinz, 5, 91, 101, 118
Schlange-Schöningen, Hans, 99
Schleswig-Holstein, 1, 2, 3, 4–6, 12, 20, 72, 74, 75, 82, 83
Schleswig-Holstein Bund, 56, 58

Schröter, Carl, 99, 100
Settlement patterns, 21,
    24-25, 26
SHBLD (*Schleswig-Hol-*
    steinische Bauern- und
    Landarbeiterdemo-
    kratie). *See Landes-*
    partei
Siegfried, André, 8
Social Democratic Party.
    See SPD
Soldiers, 21, 55, 119,
    121
Soth, Max, 33
SPD (*Sozialdemokratische*
    Partei Deutschlands),
    9, 12, 14, 16, 18-19,
    21-22, 24, 27, 29, 30,
    32, 46, 58-59, 61, 78,
    86, 87, 88, 89, 90-91,
    92, 131
SRP (*Sozialistische*
    Reichspartei), 106-108
SSW (*Südschleswigscher*
    Wählerverband), 86,
    87, 96-98
Stahlhelm Westküste, 52,
    55, 64

Steffen, Jochen, 90
Steltzer, Theodor, 99,
    100
Stoltenberg, Gerhard, 7,
    11, 16, 34-36
Struve, Detlef, 101
Sweden, 48-49

Terror, use of, 8, 65,
    69, 73
Thyssen, Thyge, 55

Uhse, Bodo, 46
USPD (*Unabhängige*
    Sozialdemokratische
    Partei Deutschlands),
    22

Varain, Heinz-Josef, 7
Voting patterns. *See*
    Ecology, political,
    and Elections

Werwolf, 55, 56
Women, 131
Wulf, Peter, 7, 27

COLLEGE
LIBRARY
DISCARD

As the only area in Germany in which a majority of the voters supported the Nazi party before the Nazis seized power, Schleswig-Holstein has attracted the attention of political scientists concerned about a possible resurgence of Nazism in West Germany under the guise of the National Democratic Party of Germany. *Nazism, Neo-Nazism, and the Peasantry* is a comparative historical study of Nazi and neo-Nazi challenges to German democracy, using electoral analysis combined with interviews and an intensive examination of local history.

The author's analysis of the Nazi Party's success and the National Democratic Party's failure in rural Schleswig-Holstein begins in chapters 1 and 2 with a probing of the social origins of Nazism. Tilton reviews the literature of electoral studies and argues that these studies strongly suggest *who* voted for the Nazis, but not *why* they did so. He then marshals the available evidence to answer this latter question. Chapter 3 reviews major demographic, economic, social, and political changes in Schleswig-Holstein from the Weimar era to the postwar period. In chapter 4, the author examines how the most recent neo-Nazi party, the National Democratic Party of Germany, has fared in this changed political context. Finally, he compares the conditions for Nazi success with the present political environment and concludes that a strong fascist revival is exceedingly improbable.

This distinguished book provides the most comprehensive analysis in English of the rise of Nazism in a specific region. It offers fascinating insights into Nazi organization in rural areas, the Nazis' penetration of existing interest groups, and their use of local elections to further their cause. It also constitutes the first detailed regional and local study in English of neo-Nazism. Previous